Th

Other books by Aidan Chambers:

NOVELS
Breaktime
Dance on My Grave
Now I Know
The Toll Bridge
Postcards from No Man's Land
This Is All
Dying to Know You
Don't Talk About Love

CHILDREN'S NOVELS
Seal Secret
The Present Takers

SHORT STORIES
The Kissing Game
Dead Trouble and other Ghost Stories

AUTOBIOGRAFICTION
A Tidman Bundle

PLAYS
Johnny Salter
The Car
The Chicken Run
The Dream Cage
Only Once
Don't Talk About Love

PICTUREBOOK
Il Vermo [*The Worme*] with Peppo Bianchessi

ESSAYS AND CRITICISM
The Reluctant Reader
*Booktalk * Reading Talk*
Tell Me with The Reading Environment

Aidan Chambers

The Age Between

Personal Reflections on Youth Fiction

fp FINCHAM PRESS

First published September 2020

Published by Fincham Press
　　　　　University of Roehampton
　　　　　School of Humanities
　　　　　Roehampton Lane
　　　　　London SW15 5PH, UK
　　　　　https://fincham.press

© 2020 Aidan Chambers

Cover art and book design by Rudolf Ammann

Typeset in Source Sans Pro and Source Serif Pro

Printed and bound by by printondemand-worldwide.com

Printed in England

All rights reserved. No part of this book may be reprinted or reproduced or utilised in any form or by any electronic, mechanical, or other means, now known or hereafter invented, including photocopying and recording, or in any information storage or retrieval system, without permission in writing from the publishers.

A catalogue record for this book is available from the British Library.

ISBN 978-1-9161214-0-9

1. Youth fiction; 2. Adolescence; 3. Teenagers; 4. Creative writing; 5. Literary criticism

CONTENTS

Foreword by Alison Waller..1

Beginnings and History...5
    Chapter 1: Beginnings..7
    Chapter 2: What's in a name?......................................19
    Chapter 3: Holden & Cecile...25
    Chapter 4: History..37
    Chapter 5: Twain as Huck..47

Defining Youth and Youth Literature...................................61
    Chapter 6: Marks of Youth...63
    Chapter 7: Youth and the Liminal................................85
    Chapter 8: Recognition...91
    Chapter 9: The Adolescent in the Adult........................97

Narrative Strategies...105
    Chapter 10: Infusion...107
    Chapter 11: How to do More with the First Person......113
    Chapter 12: The Third Person...................................119
    Chapter 13: Ways of Telling.......................................123

Closure...149
    Chapter 14: And Now?..151
    Interview...155

FOREWORD

I came to Aidan Chambers' fiction for young people late.

By the time I read *Postcards from No Man's Land*, which was published in 1999, I was just beyond the age Chambers calls 'youthhood' and was busy turning my doctoral thesis on teenage fiction into an academic book. I had encountered his innovative novel *Breaktime* (1978) during my studies, but it was *Postcards from No Man's Land* that really touched me as a reader and showed me how vital a bond could be created between textual youth, remembered youth, and lived youth.

My experiences of adolescence were very different from those of the seventeen-year-old hero of that novel. Jacob travels to Amsterdam and discovers that the fluid identity of the city and its rich and troubled history reflect something of his own emerging sense of identity. Jacob's personal journey is given further meaning and depth by a parallel story about a tragic wartime romance that reveals his secret family history. The whole thing felt incredibly exotic to a young woman from the Home Counties of England with a conventional background, who never went further than Norfolk as a teenager. And yet I recognised my own uncertainties and passions in Jacob and saw how I might have had similar adventures, given the chance.

Besides, who could not fall in love with Amsterdam after reading *Postcards*, a narrative in which the sophisticated urban landscape comes to life and fizzes with cultural resonances? As soon as I could afford it, I took a weekend trip to Amsterdam to stand in front of Rembrandt's portrait of his son Titus in the Rijksmuseum, and replay the scene in which

Jacob recognises his own features in a seventeenth-century work of art.

Chambers has a knack of getting under the skin of young characters who are in equal measure a mixture of dreams, anxiety, potential and pretention. But he also refuses to separate off those individuals aged thirteen to twenty-five – what he calls 'the age between' – from the rest of the world. Having written and published for this audience, taught them, and analysed their literary counterparts, he has retained a sense of the clear threads that bind them to their ageing companions in life. As a young reader, and even more as a returning reader in middle life, I was moved by his representation in *Postcards* of Geertrui, the elderly Dutch woman with a vibrant past, who still has much to offer in her dying days. A more recent novel, *Dying to Know You* (2011), tells a story through the correspondence between a contemporary teenage character and an ageing author, and manages to portray both with compassion and sharp observational skill. Anyone interested in adolescence, the history of youth fiction, creative writing, and readers' responses to literature will also find much to delight in this collection.

This knack of seeing life from a variety of angles is evident in the collection of personal and critical essays that follows. It is clear that Chambers' extraordinary ability to view human beings in such detail and with such range stems from his prolific reading and continued engagement with the practice and theory of creative writing. It will be a treat for anyone who has ever read his novels, heard his talks, taught from his ideas, or framed their thinking about literature for young people with his insights. They will gain a deeper understanding of Chambers' craft and his investment in the history and traditions of writing for and about youth, and they will discover that throughout his professional writing career he has been in constant dialogue with literary figures from Huckleberry Finn, Anne Frank, Holden Caulfield, to the heroes and heroines of school stories, young adult fiction, and

Shakespeare's plays.

The Age Between includes a call to action. It is a book designed to generate discussion and debate, particularly on the matter of what constitutes a canon of youth fiction. I'm delighted, then, that the collection concludes with a lively interview with academic Dr Deborah Cogan Thacker, in which Chambers delves further into literary theory and philosophical ideas as he discusses the shape, purpose and future of this literature. He considers it to be a living tradition; one that deserves a proper history as well as an ongoing and vibrant contemporary practice. Not many are better placed than he to offer this starting point.

– *Alison Waller*, University of Roehampton

BEGINNINGS AND HISTORY

CHAPTER 1
BEGINNINGS

I started writing youth fiction because of a headache.

The headache occurred after I collapsed onto the kitchen floor one night in November 1963. At the time I was a teacher of English in a co-ed secondary modern, one of the schools established in Britain by the 1944 Education Act for so-called non-academic eleven- to fifteen-year-olds, who made up about sixty per cent of the adolescent population. Most secondary modern schools were later converted into comprehensives.

Among other duties I was responsible for the school's library and drama classes. Being in charge of drama meant putting on an annual full-scale, nothing-spared play for five December evenings before an audience of pupils, teachers, parents, relatives, friends, neighbours, and anyone else who could be lured to attend and was prepared to be charmed.

We'd been rehearsing for four months. The day of my collapse we'd suffered a disastrous first dress rehearsal, beginning at 4.30pm and finally disintegrating to a dishevelled stop a few hours later. Just about everything that could have gone wrong had gone wrong, as my company of fifty or so early teens battled their way through an English adaptation of Eugene Labiche's five-act farce, *The Italian Straw Hat*. The farce that evening was not the one intended by the author but the spectacle of our calamitous incompetence in every department of the production.

Why on earth, I wondered as I made my exhausted way home, had I chosen a play so inappropriate to the age, talents and experience of both life and theatre of my ever-willing but now downcast pupils? What would be appropriate? What would suit them and be right for them?

I had an inkling of the answer. I'd been thinking about it for years, in connection with plays and with the fiction I was responsible for providing and encouraging them to read.

I was still tussling with these questions by the time I got home and collapsed semi-conscious onto the kitchen floor.

I'd recovered enough to go to work next day – as you do, because you have to. The second dress rehearsal a few days later was accomplished without irreparable hitches, and the five performances passed off with reasonable success. What did not pass off was a headache, which felt like a tight fist squeezing my brain while a sharp knife sliced it open, an operation without anaesthetic.

It began the day after I collapsed. By the end of January I'd had enough, and consulted a doctor. A late-middle-aged GP of the kind no longer to be found, who, it was rumoured, was fond of the bottle and was never available during Cheltenham Race week, performed the usual tests – checking blood pressure, peering into ears, nose and throat, listening to heart and lungs, testing reflexes, checking my abdomen, asking if I smoked (at that time ten a day; I gave up for good in 1973) and drank booze (very little), that kind of thing – and then inquiring about my daily routine, spare-time activities, and work.

That done, he gave me what my mother would have called an old-fashioned look of the sort that makes you feel you've been rumbled, although you're not sure what for, and said, 'I can't find anything wrong with you. If you think I'm going to tell you you're overworking, I'm not. I work just as hard as you. And I don't want to know what's going on in your head. That's for a priest or a shrink. It's none of my business. But I will say this. There's something missing in your life, young man, and when you find out what it is and do something about it the headaches will stop. In the meantime I'll give you some pills that should help.'

As soon as he said it, I knew what was missing, in the way you admit to yourself only when someone else faces you with it; something you've known for a long time but have ignored because you don't want to deal with the consequences. But for two months I did nothing about it. I took the pills and hoped the headache would go away. It didn't. The pills dulled the pain to a blur. They also dulled everything else to a blur that fogged my thoughts, my feelings, my memory, my energy, even now and then my hearing and sight, my dreams as well, and I won't even mention my torpid libido. After a month I was going about like a zombie, and pupils and colleagues were beginning to notice. After two months I could hardly get out of a chair, my lessons passed with only a vague awareness of teaching them, and everyone was looking at me askance.

One day at the end of the second month I was in such a bad state, I was taken home by my attentive boss and told to stay there until I felt better. I was off work for a week. I finished that month's allocation of pills and collected the next month's supply, but deliberately didn't open the bottle. I'd decided to give up on drugs and do what I knew had to be done. I still have the bottle wrapped in the paper in which it was handed to me by the pharmacist. A reminder, a souvenir, and a talisman.

I learned much later, by the way, that the pills were a lethal potion, a tranquilising concoction banned some years later because of its injurious effects when taken over an extended period, such as memory loss, mental disorders, erratic behaviour, and unfortunate pathological changes in personality. I'd had a narrow escape.

Instead of taking the pills, I stole an exercise book from school and started to write both a story and a play with my pupils in mind as their characters and readers.

I'll try to explain why.

At the age of fifteen I decided I would be a writer of literary novels and plays without anything in my background to explain it. For the following ten years I wrote poems and stories that I tried to get published, but they were always rejected. True, while training as a teacher I wrote a play performed at the college one-act play festival. It was hobbled by the pretentious title *Everyman's Everybody* and was described by a friend as a poor man's *Waiting for Godot*, which happened to receive its first English performance that same year but which I hadn't seen, and hadn't even heard of its author.

The comparison forced me to face the first lesson you learn as a published writer: how to survive the poisonous pill of a well-aimed dismissive review.

The authorial failures multiplied during my first job, three years teaching at a grammar school in a seaside town. I gave up trying when I started my second job, which eventually lasted seven happy years, at the aforementioned secondary modern in a small town in rural Gloucestershire. By then I enjoyed working as a teacher so much, and the work was so time-consuming and emotionally demanding – or rather I made it so because I loved it – that the attempt to become a successful writer did not feel like it was worth the effort and the disappointments. It seemed obvious I hadn't the talent or whatever else it takes to become a published writer. So I gave up. But I soon learned it's much harder and more painful to abandon what amounts to an obsessive compulsion than it is to suffer the pains of the obsession. I hadn't learned yet that failure is inevitable. It's what life is about.

My collapse on the kitchen floor was the suppressed compulsion hitting back, an existential crisis warning of worse to come if I didn't accept the fact that, whether I liked it or not, I was a compulsive writer. And somehow or other the doctor had spotted the nature of the crisis. Something missing. Put it back and you'll be well again.

In the drug-induced blur, two realities combined to save me from the medical poison, and myself.

First of all, I was struggling to find fiction that my so-called 'non-academic' and reluctant readers would willingly read. I hadn't been able to find more than a handful of books. Not enough to satisfy a variety of tastes and encourage persistence. Second of all, here I was falling ill because I wanted to be a writer, but had given up. If I didn't try again and keep on trying I really would go off my head and end up dead.

That which was missing had to be put back. Therefore, I asked myself through the fog, why not attempt to write the kind of fiction I couldn't find for my failing pupils? If I failed, at least we would fail together. After all, I knew what they would read if I could find it, because they had told me. At my request, they'd even made lists of the essential features. The stories must be short (no more than about 30,000 words, from the examples they showed me). They must be about people like them doing the kind of things they did, could do, or would like to do. They didn't want 'any of that historical fiction' (which was published in quantity at the time), it was boring; nor 'that fantasy stuff' (also published a lot then) because 'we don't believe in them and they are silly, and they're not even science fiction because it isn't as good as Doctor Who on the telly'.

They wanted stories about real life. Their real lives. They wanted the stories to be set in places like where they lived. And they wanted them to be about now.

As it happened, I'd found three short novels that did fit the bill. I'd read them aloud to all four years, eleven- to fifteen-year-olds. Many of the students went on to read the books again for themselves. And they asked for more of the same, which was the best sign of success. But I couldn't find more of the same.

These benchmark books were: *Gumble's Yard* by John Rowe Townsend, a story about working-class youngsters up against it and surviving on their own in a northern industrial town; *Jim Starling* by Wallace Hildick, an amusing story set mainly in a secondary modern school, which included a comic scene in an art class so like the one my pupils attended that they rolled about with laughter. And *Fifteen* by Beverly Cleary, the runaway favourite with both boys and girls in all four years, a funny and touching American story of the bumbling attempts of a teenage dogs' meat delivery boy to date a girl he fancies.

Apart from the contents, *Fifteen* possessed a particular advantage over the other two. It was the only one in paperback. And the cover was astutely designed to appeal to teenagers – girls especially – who avidly read the magazines published for them. I'd already found that if I placed two copies of a book in the library, one in hardback and one in paperback, the paperback would be borrowed but not the hardback. Paperbacks were what was then called 'hip', and would now be called 'cool'.

A sunny weekend in March 1964. My tranquilisers abandoned. Exercise book and pencil at the ready. A title: *First Date*. Characters based on some of my pupils. Setting: a small town and a school like ours. A story that took its cue from *Fifteen* and was based on the teenage boy-girl goings on I'd heard about from my pupils or remembered from the confusions, embarrassments, unsatisfied desires, fluctuating moods, dispiriting calamities, and up and down excitements of my own adolescence. I wanted it to include the kind of gritty realities that *Gumble's Yard* described but *Fifteen* didn't.

A year later, a sympathetic publisher I'd met at a conference of teachers and school librarians read the finished typescript. He wrote a long and gentle letter explaining why he wouldn't publish it and advised me to stow this attempt away in my bottom drawer and start another. It was evident I was a writer, he said, but this was an apprentice book. He was sure someone would publish it and to go ahead if I wanted, but he was equally sure that if I did I'd regret it later in what he was also sure would be a successful career.

At the time I was furious with him, upset, disappointed, humiliated. I was sorry I'd asked him to read the wretched thing. To make the rejection worse, this wasn't even the kind of writing I'd been attempting to produce for years; proper, grown-up, literary fiction, not teenage pap. I couldn't bear to look at the typescript again. I felt like incinerating it. But I didn't. Even at that moment, a moment of anger that lasted at least a month, something in me prevented annihilation. Something said that as a writer you must never waste anything, everything is or can be valuable, whatever you've written is part of you, do not destroy parts of you. I hadn't scrapped any of the other unpublished failures, why scrap this one? I knew, but didn't want to acknowledge, that I'd have to try again. There was no choice.

I also knew there was something different from all the others about this attempt. I knew who this book was for. And why. In other words, I'd found a readership and a voice suited to it and a story that had a purpose. All I needed to do was catch my breath, screw my courage to the sticking place, and start again.

A second lesson in a writer's life: the purging torment of rejection. Answer: get over it and carry on. One of those factors that sort out the cannot-help-but-be-a-writer from the would-be-but-aren't.

The publisher's name was Antony Kamm, who headed up Brockhampton Press, the only publishing house then dedicated solely to books for children and what was called 'older children'. The 'older children's books' were soon to be identified as 'teenage books', which the Americans were already calling 'young adult books', but were not yet an accepted category in Britain. I owe Antony a huge debt. He was right. I'm sorry I never published anything with him; a few years later he left publishing and Brockhampton Press disappeared as an imprint. Antony's mother, Josephine Kamm, by the way, wrote one of the books of the kind I was looking for. *Young Mother* caused a ripple of controversy when it came out in 1965 because it dealt with the then taboo subject of unmarried teenage pregnancy in a story that respected and did not condescend to its youth readers.

By 1968 I'd written and published two short novels for my pupils, *Marle* and *Cycle Smash*, as well as three plays performed by them, *Johnny Salter*, *The Car* and *The Chicken Run*. At the same time I was setting up Topliners with Macmillan Education, a series of original stories for teenagers by writers who held views similar to mine about what was needed. The books were published in paperback, an innovation at the time when origination in paperback was pretty much unknown. They were successful, and my other public work associated with fiction, education, and the young – reviewing, journalism, speaking at conferences and meetings of teachers and librarians, appearances on radio and television, organising and tutoring in-service courses – grew to the point that I couldn't keep up with full-time teaching. It was a hard choice. To say I enjoyed teaching is an understatement. But the quality of my teaching was suffering because of time spent on other activities. I decided that, now I was published at last, if I didn't give myself entirely to what I'd wanted to do since I was fifteen, I would ever after resent myself for not taking the chance.

A third lesson. An unforgiveable determination against all wise reason, regardless of anyone else, and come what may, is necessary if you're to become a committed writer. A kind of arrogance.

I went on writing and publishing for the young until 1975. Writing for a known audience, taking into account whatever limitations and preferences of language, form and subject I thought appropriate to a teenaged readership.

Why nothing more for the young after 1975? What happened? Not another physical collapse. More of a psychic collapse, a collapse of the will.

By then I'd been a self-employed writer for seven years. I was no longer in daily contact with the readers for whom I was writing. And though I'd published books for them – ghost stories, for example, anthologies of short stories, information books – I'd written no novels or plays since the late 1960s. I hadn't because, whatever anyone else thought of them, they didn't satisfy me.

In the summer of 1975 I decided it was time to try and write another novel. I had a story in mind. For days I stared at a blank page. But nothing came. Not because there was nothing there, nothing in my head. There was. But I couldn't make myself write one word. It was as if my writerly self had gone on strike.

To understand what happened next, it's necessary to know that almost everything I'd published so far had been written directly onto a typewriter. For two reasons. First, I liked the click of the keys in the rhythm of composition; the sound of purposeful busyness, the announcement of work being done. Second and just as important: somehow or other, probably from reading interviews with contemporary writers and their biographies, I'd got it into my head that the best modern writers always used typewriters. Ernest Hemingway, for example, used to start his day by sharpening pencils to get him going, then wrote a few words in very large letters till the flow gathered pace, when he turned to his typewriter and set to work properly.

Fourth lesson of being a writer. At the beginning you need models. All skills, everything we do, we learn by imitation. But beware, see lesson five below.

Here I am, then, staring at a blank sheet of paper wound into a typewriter for days on end. Quite literally unable to make my fingers work. Finally in desperation, hoping a change of circumstances would help, I forced myself to pick up a pad of paper and a pen, sit in a comfortable arm chair away from my desk, and after noting the time and taking a deep breath made a deal with myself to write down the first words that came into my head and go on until I told myself to stop.

The first words were '"Literature is crap,"' said Morgan.'

Those who have read it will know these are not the first words of *Breaktime*, but they turn up on the second page in a dialogue between two seventeen-year-old boys; Ditto, who is the focalising first-person narrator, and his friend Morgan.

My memory is that this spontaneous improvisation went on for about an hour and twenty minutes. I read the result and hadn't a clue what the boys were talking about or what was going on or what would happen next. I'd never before been so unknowing, so unplanned, so completely in the dark when writing something.

A few days went by, sitting at my desk and staring at the typewriter. Nothing. So a repeat performance: chair, pad of paper, pen: Go! Ditto carried on telling his story. When the words dried up again, I decided to type out what I'd scrawled. I found I was revising as I typed, adding, cutting, changing words, sentences, inventing more. And behold: the flow began! First draft handwritten, second and further drafts on a typewriter. Hone and refine, hone and refine, back and forth. Constant revision.

The book was three years in the making from start to publication by the Bodley Head in 1978. *Breaktime* taught me what I needed to know about myself as a writer, how I write best, what I need to write, and why. Not that I could express it clearly at the time, either to myself or to anyone else. That came later, helped by Roland Barthes when I found his famous essay 'Authors and writers', a difference I explain in the chapter 'Ways of Telling'.

Breaktime taught me the fifth lesson of being an author. Though you need models to emulate and imitate at the start, you also need to find out how you work best. With what tools: pen or pencil on paper; typing on a word processor? Thinking out what you want to write before writing it or thinking by writing? Where? In a special place or anywhere? When? Morning, afternoon, evening, night, any time? At set times or not? Only when you feel like it or by following a strict discipline whether you feel like it or not? Food, drink, sleep, exercise? With background music or none, in silence or where there is ambient noise, in a public place (library, café, park, on a train) or in isolated privacy? All and more come into the formula.

The fact is, there are no rules about authorship, except the rules you make for yourself. And this one: the need to read constantly and deeply. We belong to a tradition. By studying other authors' work we learn from them.

But study all you like, it is only by writing that you learn how to do it in your own way.

At the time of writing this I am eighty-five. The old are incorrigibly reflective. It is as if a switch has been turned on. You can't help looking back, reviewing what you've done, what you didn't do and wished you had, what was good and right, what could have been done better, what was embarrassingly bad and is regretted.

This book is my personal reflection on youth fiction, what I've learned from reading and writing it, what I wish I'd learned earlier because it would have helped me write better, and what I now understand only with the benefit of hindsight.

Which leads me to end this chapter with the sixth lesson I've learned about writing. You need the energy of delusion. This wonderful phrase is Tolstoy's. When he couldn't get going with *Anna Karenina* he told his friend and editor N. Strakhov in April 1878, 'Everything seems to be ready for writing – for fulfilling my earthly duty, what's missing is the urge to believe in myself, the belief in the importance of my task, I'm lacking the energy of delusion; an earthly, spontaneous energy that's impossible to invent. And it's impossible to begin without it.'

As an author you can only do your work when you're able to delude yourself into the belief that what you're writing is worthwhile, that it's necessary to yourself and might be of some use to others. I've always found it hard to urge belief in myself. So why go on? Fernando Pessoa gives the best answer I know of in his masterpiece *The Book of Disquiet*. One of the great tragedies, he observes, 'is to execute a work and then realise, once it's finished, that it's not any good. The tragedy is especially great when one realises that the work is the best he could have done. But to write a work, knowing beforehand that it's bound to be flawed and imperfect; to see while writing it that it's flawed and imperfect – this is the height of spiritual torture and humiliation.' But Pessoa goes on writing, 'Because I still haven't learned to practise completely the renunciation that I preach … I have to write, as if I were carrying out a punishment. And the greatest punishment is to know that whatever I write will be futile, flawed and uncertain'.

References

Fernando Pessoa, *The Book of Disquiet*, ed. & trans. Richard Zenith, Allen Lane The Penguin Press, 2001. Page 200.

Lev Tolstoy quoted in Viktor Shklovsky, *Energy of Delusion: A Book on Plot*, trans. Sushhan Avagyan, Dalkey Archive Press, 2007. Page 36.

CHAPTER 2
WHAT'S IN A NAME?

> *I would there were no age between ten and three-and-twenty, or that youth would sleep out the rest; for there is nothing in between but getting wenches with child, wronging the ancientry, stealing, fighting.*
>
> – Shepherd, *The Winter's Tale*, William Shakespeare

Why do I prefer the term 'youth fiction'?

When I began my career in the 1950s the usual British term was 'books for older children', there being little recognition by publishers of the separate nature of adolescence; that it was not merely an extension of childhood and therefore needed fiction addressed to that age group. During the 1960s the difference began to be acknowledged and the term 'books for teenagers' became the norm. The Americans were already calling them 'young adult books', the term now most commonly used everywhere. But in my opinion, none of these will do, for these reasons:

The term 'teenage' restricts us to the years between thirteen and nineteen. But for some, perhaps most people, their youth extends beyond the age of nineteen. And for many who are teenaged, the word carries pejorative cultural baggage and is often used disparagingly by adults who are not too fond of that age group. I know someone who, half-joking, calls them JDs – juvenile delinquents.

Some specialists ascribe 'young adult' to the years between

eighteen and thirty-five, in which period, they claim, human beings reach the peak of their biological capacities and become fully adult. The influential developmental psychologist Erik Erikson, for example, ascribes eighteen to thirty-nine as the years of young adulthood. But besides this, the term suggests that the person is already an adult, which confuses the issue. The biological technical term 'adolescent' has an unappealing, clinical tone to it and is hobbled by the same limit as 'teenage'. According to Erikson, it is the period between thirteen and seventeen. Best, then, to avoid the word.

Which leaves us with the word 'youth'. This has a long pedigree with roots in Latin *juventus*, Gothic *junda*, Old High German *iugund*, Old Frisian *jogethe*, and Old English *gepgoth*. And there are precedents. The United Nations General Assembly settled on the ages of youth being between fifteen and twenty-four. Advertising companies work to the same definition. The World Bank adds a year, fifteen to twenty-five. The British Commonwealth Youth Programme works with fifteen- to twenty-nine-year-olds. Shakespeare's Shepherd allots this busy time to the years between ten to twenty-three.

What we can say is that 'youth' identifies a period of human life between childhood and mature adulthood.

And as we use 'childhood' as the noun denoting the condition of being a child, and 'adulthood' as the noun denoting the condition of being an adult, I propose to use the noun 'youthhood' when referring to the condition of being in 'the age between' childhood and adulthood.

In his book *Signs of Childness in Children's Books* Peter Hollindale revived the old English term 'childness', meaning the quality of being a child. Polixenese in Shakespeare's *The Winter's Tale* describes with moving eloquence how his son,

> If at home, sir,
> He's all my exercise, my mirth, my matter:
> Now my sworn friend, and then mine enemy;
> My parasite, my soldier, statesman, all:

> He makes a July's day short as December;
> And with his varying childness cures in me
> Thought that would thick my blood.

Following Hollindale's lead, I propose to use the term 'youthness' for the quality – or rather I'd say the qualities – of being a youth, the nature of which I example in the chapter 'Marks of Youth', which dwells on how youth fiction must deal with the well-known biological changes that occur during youthhood, changes which nowadays the neuro- and especially the brain scientists are reporting in rapidly increasing detail.

But Shakespeare and other writers described these qualities long before modern scientists got to work. Lev Tolstoy, for example, wrote about some of the determining features we've all experienced in his Diary on January 2, 1852, when he was twenty-four and could talk about the nature of youthhood while it was still presently alive in him and actively forming his adult character:

> For all young people there is a time when they have no firm ideas about things – no rules – and are drawing them up, both the one and the other. At this time they usually shun practical interests and live in a moral world. This transitional period I call youth. For some people youth lasts longer than for others. There are even people who always remain young, and others who have never been young. What does the length of this period depend on? It would seem that since, as I said, young people at this time are busy trying to draw up firm ideas about things, and rules, then the cleverer the young person is, the quicker this period ought to pass: he will draw up rules for himself and live by them. But in reality it is just the opposite. The practical side of life demands our attention more and more the further we progress through it; but the more inclination a man has towards reflection (and so finds moral pleasure in it), the more

he tries to put this transitional period of time behind him; but in order to draw up correct ideas about things and correct rules for life, a whole lifetime of reflection is not enough; although he advances along this path, necessity requires him to stop drawing up rules and to act according to whatever ones have already been drawn up. And so when we start out on our practical life, we all begin to act on the basis of those imperfect and incomplete rules and ideas which necessity has found us with.

Tolstoy touches on some of the existential features that are particularly prevalent in the age between, especially the tussle between idealism and practicality, and the desire to be free and self-determining while at the same time facing the confining rules and customs of everyday life. I'm amused how, at the age of twenty-four, he speculates that a whole lifetime is not enough to draw up correct ideas about life, something he discovered from his own experience to be disturbingly true. That being so, we might say, once a youth always a youth.

To sum up:
By youth I mean the biological period between roughly thirteen and roughly twenty-five years of age, a state of being with its own identifying and particular features which are dominant in that period, and which can be re-engaged at other times after that, either temporarily or permanently. What these features are I'll come to and set out why it's my contention that, because youth is a period distinctly different from childhood and adulthood, it not only needs but deserves a distinctive and different literature devoted to it: stories, novels, poetry, plays, history, auto- and biography, and other kinds of texts based on narrative.

As well as all this, just as there is a history of our understanding of the age between, there is a history of books published for readers who were no longer children but could not be called adult, and we need to attend to it if we are to understand what has been achieved and what can now be done to help youth fiction evolve. Before I thought of it as separate, and studied its history myself, two novels interested me as a teacher of literature, and then later were instructive models. I turn to these in the next chapter.

References
Peter Hollindale, *Signs of Childness in Children's Books*, Thimble Press, 1997. Page 45.

William Shakespeare, *The Winter's Tale, The Complete Works*, Riverside Second Edition, Houghton Mifflin, 1997. III.iii. 59-63, I.ii. 165-171

Lev Tolstoy, *Diaries Vol. 1: 1847-1894*, ed. & trans. R.F. Christian, Faber & Faber, 2010, Page 41.

CHAPTER 3
HOLDEN & CECILE

In the late 1950s two novels were published very successfully in Penguin paperback editions. At the time, I was in my first job as a twenty-three-year-old teacher of English and Drama in an all-boys' grammar school. One of the books was controversial and very popular with my pupils. The other, of which my pupils were unaware, was widely praised by critics as a remarkably accomplished study of an eighteen-year-old girl, all the more impressive because it was written by a schoolgirl of the same age.

When, for reasons I've explained, I began to write fiction with my teenaged pupils in mind, I reread both books to find out what I might learn from them; what features might distinguish a novel written entirely about, and only from, the perspective of youthhood by someone who was still a youth, as against a similar novel written by a mature, adult author.

One was written by an adult American male. The other by a teenaged French female. Both were published as adult novels. One was taken over by the young. The other was promoted by the literary establishment (reviewers, academics, critics) as a precociously mature work of adult literature. Both stories are confined to the first-person consciousness of their adolescent protagonists, one a sixteen-year-old male, the other a seventeen-year-old female.

The American novel was *The Catcher in the Rye* by J. D. Salinger. The French novel was *Bonjour Tristesse* by Françoise Sagan.

The Catcher in the Rye was published in the US on July 16,

1951. Its author, Jerome David Salinger, was thirty-two. He had worked on his novel for ten years, elaborating it from a short story, 'Slight Rebellion off Madison'. Famously reclusive and antagonistic toward interviewers, he was not always so retiring. In 1953 he told a high-school newspaper that *Catcher* was 'sort of' autobiographical and that his youth had been very like Holden's. Though an immediate runaway success in the US, it became a long-time bestseller in Britain only after youth readers adopted it, when the Penguin paperback edition was published in 1958.

How did *Catcher* arouse and retain the attention of the young? We have a first-hand account of this happening to Ian Hamilton, who became a notable British critic and poet. He was seventeen, already a committed literary reader, when he came across a copy of *Catcher* in his local bookshop. The book exercised such a permanent hold on him that late in his career he set out to write a biography of Salinger. But he was thwarted by his hero's resolute opposition, which was pursued through a series of court cases that ended with a decision against Hamilton, preventing even the conventionally acceptable 'fair use' of quotations from Salinger's letters. Hamilton revised his book, paraphrasing the passages he was not allowed to quote, and turned it into a biographer's detective story titled *In Search of J.D. Salinger*. In it, he describes *Catcher*'s effect on his teenaged self.

He was seventeen when he found a copy of the book and was so gripped, he carried it with him everywhere. He thought it funnier, more emotionally moving, and what he called more 'right' than any other novel he had read. He would persuade prospective friends, especially girls, to read it. It they didn't 'get it' they were dropped.

It was the famous first sentence that caught him. He thought it 'audacious'. Not only that:

> ...*The Catcher*'s colloquial balancing act is not just something boldly headlined on page one: It is wonderfully

sustained from first to last. And so too, it seemed to me, was everything else in the book: its humour, its pathos, and, above all, its wisdom, the certainty of its world view. Holden Caulfield knew the difference between the phony and the true. As I did. *The Catcher* was the book that taught me what I ought already to have known: that literature can speak for you, not just to you. It seemed to me 'my book'.

When I asked my pupils in 1958 why they liked *Catcher* so much, the reasons they gave were versions of this. In sum, it was the very strong, colloquial, first-person voice of a rebellious teenager, combined with what Hamilton calls the 'message', that did the trick. The result was the experience often called 'an epiphany': a showing forth, a recognition of one's existence validated, in this case, by a work of fiction.

I empathised with this because it matched my own experience when, at the age of fifteen, I read D.H. Lawrence's *Sons and Lovers*, the influence of which was so strong it created in me the ambition to be a writer of a similar kind of novel. But I have to confess there was something about *Catcher* that made me uneasy. Not the voice, which, as Hamilton says, is 'wonderfully sustained from first to last'. I could understand why it caught and gripped the attention. My unease had something to do with the 'message', which Hamilton calls 'its wisdom, the certainty of its world view', and which he asserts is wonderfully sustained 'above all'.

What, I wondered, is this 'wisdom'? What is it that Holden Caulfield knows and speaks so compellingly to youth readers? We know what Holden likes. Golf, tennis, and fencing. And reading. (*The Great Gatsby, Out of Africa, The Return of the Native, A Farewell to Arms*, and *Romeo and Juliet* are mentioned.) He's also an abundant drinker and smoker. But what does he care about?

'Phony' is one of Holden's favourite words, meaning hypocritical, pretentious, insincere, fake. Every adult he mentions is phony except his favourite English teacher, Mr Antolini. But even he falls from grace and joins the ranks of the phonies when, after being given a bed for the night, Holden wakes to find Mr Antolini 'in the dark and all, and was sort of petting me or patting me on the goddam head'. At first it seems that Holden's older brother D.B. is admirable. But we quickly learn he isn't because he's writing scripts in Hollywood. So he doesn't count among the elect either.

Phoniness is not the preserve of adults, however. Just about everyone Holden's own age, in school or out, is tainted. I've wondered if Holden ever asked himself whether he might be phony himself, but can find no sign of such self-inquiry. Who isn't phony? His twelve-year-old sister, Phoebe. And some 'kids' about her age who Holden comes across now and then during his wanderings in New York City. It's in Holden's encounters with 'kids', and in one of the scenes with Phoebe, that what Holden cares about and the significance of the book's title – its 'message' – is made clear.

The first of these revelatory moments occurs in Chapter Sixteen, when Holden sees a man and a woman who 'looked sort of poor' coming from church, walking along 'not paying any attention to their kid' of about six years old. As he walked along the side of the road, he was singing 'in a pretty little voice', 'If a body catch a body coming through the rye'. Cars were rushing by, brakes screaming as they tried to avoid him. His parents took no notice. As Holden watched and listened, the boy singing 'for the hell of it' made him feel better, less depressed. To Holden, kids – who seem to be people below the age of thirteen – are the only people who are not phony.

In Chapter Twenty-Two, Holden sneaks into his parents' house at night to be with Phoebe. Towards the end of this long scene Holden says to his sister, 'You know what I'd like to be? I mean if I had a goddam choice?' And tells her:

'You know that song "If a body catch a body comin'

through the rye"? I'd like – '

'It's "If a body meet a body coming through the rye"!' old Phoebe said. 'It's a poem. By Robert Burns.'

'I know it's a poem by Robert Burns.'

She was right though. It is 'If a body meet a body coming through the rye'. I didn't know it then, though.

'I thought it was "If a body catch a body",' I said. 'Anyway, I keep picturing all these little kids playing some game in this big field of rye and all. Thousands of little kids, and nobody's around – nobody big, I mean – except me. And I'm standing on the edge of some crazy cliff. What I have to do, I have to catch everybody if they start to go over the cliff – I mean if they're running and they don't look where they're going I have to come out from somewhere and catch them. That's all I'd do all day. I'd just be the catcher in the rye and all. I know it's crazy, but that's the only thing I'd really like to be.'

Holden's Freudian slip – 'catch' for 'meet' – is revealing. What he 'really wants' is to live in a world peopled only by children, except for himself, who would be their guardian, their 'catcher' – their keeper and saviour. Peter Pan comes to mind. What Holden wants is to live in a Neverland of innocence where the kids are always 'nice and polite' and Holden is the only 'big' person, and no one is phony.

Adults are phony, or negligent, or untrustworthy.

Children are honest and true.

Therefore the best thing, the thing to want, is never to grow up.

This, it seems to me, is the 'message', the 'wisdom' of Holden.

'The novel,' wrote Milan Kundera, 'is a meditation on existence, seen through imaginary characters.' The meditations we call novels, and in fact all stories of every kind, are narrative variations on what happens, to whom, where, when, and why. And the question 'Why?' is the heart of the matter.

'A beautiful young woman threw herself under a train' is a statement of what happens and to whom, but it goes nowhere unless we are told why she did it. It takes Tolstoy most of *Anna Karenina* to tell us. We are fascinated not so much by what people do as by the reasons for their behaviour. Often, when we know why, we wonder whether they might have behaved differently, and how we would have behaved in similar circumstances, and why. We wonder how they – and we – might have behaved differently and better.

'Nothing is more important,' Wittgenstein suggested, 'for teaching us to understand the concepts we have than constructing fictitious ones.' In other words, all stories are moral systems. They propose meanings and possibilities, reasons and motives, better rather than worse ways of living, whether their authors mean them to or not. They engage in suppositions. They ask: 'What if?' And tell what happens if those possibilities are enacted, and what the results might be.

'Telling a story,' wrote Paul Ricoeur, 'is deploying an imaginary space for thought experiments in which moral judgement operates in a hypothetical mode.' In his monumental three-volume *Time and Narrative*, in *Oneself as Another*, and elsewhere in his extraordinary body of work, Ricoeur refines this understanding of stories as moral systems. He makes a distinction between ethics and morality. Ethics, he says, is the aim of an accomplished life. We aim for betterment or worthwhileness or purpose or justifiable achievement. Morality is the attempt to achieve this aim by taking action in what Ricoeur calls the norms of behaviour. An ethical aim in life can only be expressed and achieved by passing through 'the sieve of the norm' – in other words, by doing something. Ricoeur suggests that whenever in life we come to an impasse in the practice of our moral norms, our actions, we have to submit to the ethical aim we have set for ourselves. We have to think again and reorientate our course of action.

This very aporia – this puzzling problem of aim set against behaviour – is the impasse at the end of *Catcher*.

My reading of what Hamilton calls the 'message' of *Catcher* is that Holden's aim is to live his Neverland life alone with children. But as his story takes him through the actions, the 'sieve of the norms' of the life he finds himself living because of the circumstances of his birth and background, he comes to a puzzled halt in the very short last chapter of the novel. In it he says that he doesn't want to tell us what happened when he went home and what he's supposed to do next, because he's 'sorry I told so many people'.

Why? Because 'all I know is, I sort of miss everybody I told about … It's funny. Don't ever tell anybody anything. If you do, you start missing everybody'.

It seems to me that the so-far loquacious Holden is finally reduced to silence because he cannot face a truth, a profound wisdom, he would rather not acknowledge. No man is an island. You can only be yourself, you can only become yourself, in an active relationship of caring attention given to and received from others. If Holden has learned this, he isn't able to say it. Realising this 'wisdom', understanding this 'message', which Holden can't face and doesn't articulate, is left for the reader to work out.

I wonder if Salinger intended this? Perhaps I'm uneasy about *Catcher* because I can't persuade myself that he did.

This, at least, is my reading of the story. But I know most people disagree with me. For many, like Hamilton, it's an epiphany book. For others, the convincing nature of Holden's voice, its reality and vigour, is what they admire, never mind about anything else.

I have no idea if Françoise Quoirez had read *Catcher*, though I doubt it, when at the age of eighteen she wrote *Bonjour*

Tristesse. It was published in 1954 and instantly became an international bestseller. She took Sagan as her pseudonym after the character Princesse de Sagan in Proust's *A la recherché du temps perdu*.

It's quite likely that Holden would write off Cecile, the seventeen-year-old narrating protagonist of Sagan's novel, as one of the phonies. For example, *Bonjour* begins with Cecile telling us about her father and their domestic setup, the very kind of information Holden won't give because he says it's crap and by implication too much like the old novels he regards as outdated and irrelevant.

Holden regards all adults as phony. Cecile doesn't. Quite the opposite. She remarks on the enviable maturity of Anne, the forty-year-old sophisticated woman who, given her own way, would cause a change and unsettlement in Cecile's life.

Bonjour is in chapters but also in two parts. In the second part there is a significant growth in Cecile's character, a development that doesn't happen to Holden. Part Two begins:

> I'm surprised how clearly I remember everything from that moment. I acquired an added awareness of other people and of myself. Until then I had always been spontaneous and lighthearted, but the last few days had upset me to the extent of forcing me to reflect and to look at myself with a critical eye.

Holden never makes such progress. In this essential sense, *Catcher* is static, harping on one theme, one unchanging condition, whereas *Bonjour* moves, grows, narrates an increasing understanding of the human condition.

There is also a difference in the attitude of the two characters to the people around them. Holden and Cecile are self-regarding, selfish, solipsistic, demanding of attention. But Holden is entirely inward. He looks only into himself. Cecile looks from herself outward. She asks herself how others might feel, what others might think, what others make of the circumstances in which they find themselves and which she has created.

There is another difference between the two novels. Holden is attempting an act of de-identification. He is setting himself against the adults around him by telling himself they are phony without making any attempt to understand them. He does this in order to establish himself in his own mind as different from those who would otherwise influence and guide him – parents, teachers, peers, even his own brother. He thinks it's only possible to be himself by disregarding everyone else. Cecile on the other hand does everything she can to maintain her identification with – her possession of and her possession by – her father.

Holden's weakness is his banal blindness. Cecile's weakness is her clear-eyed determination to remain attached to her father.

It seems to me there is an entirely different attitude on the part of the two authors to their stories and their characters. By their own admission the central characters are projections of themselves, reworkings of their own life-experience. Unsurprising, then, that Salinger became reclusive and preferred the company of young people. Equally unsurprising that Sagan was gregarious, hedonistic, and irresponsible all her life – drink, drugs, promiscuous sex, fast cars – but in her novels always wrote about people of her own age and charted the increasingly self-conscious and self-critical journey from youth to middle and older age.

The ethical aim of the two novels is also different. Whereas Holden would rather not grow up, Cecile wants to, but cuts herself off from doing so. One is unknowing, the other is knowing. One is unaware of what it is best to become, the other is aware of it but cannot; or rather, at the moment doesn't want to achieve it. Which leads you to expect the two stories to end differently. But they don't.

Catcher ends with Holden tongue-tied because he's found

that if you tell about people – even though they are phony – you 'start missing' them. *Bonjour* ends with Cecile living the same hedonistic, irresponsible, essentially immature life with her father she was living before Anne intruded and tried to help Cecile grow up. Though Cecile wants to grow up, wants to be as confident and assured, as sophisticated and mature as Anne, her attachment to her father is so strong it prevents her accepting Anne and the change she will cause in their lives and relationships. Anne dies as a result of Cecile's deliberate, delinquent plot to prevent the marriage to her father. Her death is both an event in the story and the metaphor of Cecile stifling her own development.

For Cecile, at the end of her story: 'that summer returns to me with all its memories. Anne, Anne, I repeat over and over again softly in the darkness. Then something rises in me that I welcome by name, with closed eyes: Bonjour tristesse.' Hello sadness. This is almost exactly Holden's realisation. 'You start missing everybody.' But at least in Cecile's sadness there is awareness of what could have been. 'An ethical identity,' Paul Ricoeur says, 'requires a person accountable for his or her acts.' As far as we know from what he tells us, Holden is never accountable – to himself or anyone else. Cecile is. She concedes her responsibility and knowingly makes an unwise moral choice.

In both stories it is left to the reader to think beyond the characters, who are stuck in the kind of exquisite aporias of life and how to live it which are so much enjoyed in narcissistic youthhood.

Is dramatic irony in play here, the kind which occurs when readers realise they know more than the characters? And if it is, is it deliberately intended by the authors or not? I suspect Sagan intends it. But whether Salinger does is open to question.

What did I discover in the two novels? That they narrate the two poles of youthhood's need. The need to be free from parental and childhood ties that get in the way of becoming what you imagine you want to be. And the need to be rooted and safe and unchangingly identified as a self given the birth conditions of your life – family history, genetic makeup, cultural background.

As an author, from the beginning I wanted my novels to depict both needs, because this seemed truer to life than only one or the other alone.

That said, it's useful to consider the formal and thematic similarities of the two novels.

Holden and Cecile appealed to youth readers because they seemed to be new voices speaking the truths of life; truths they thought had not been expressed quite like this before. The stories are told in the most conventional 'old fashioned' pre-Modernist manner. Both are told chronologically, one event leading to the next. Viktor Shklovsky in *Theory of Prose* calls this 'stepped structure' and 'step-by-step construction', which I've adapted as stepped narratives. There are no flashbacks (though there are moments of remembering) or other intrusions, no metafictive devices to disturb the straightforward progress of the narrative.

They are told in numbered chapters.

There are no subplots or diversions.

Both are narrated in the first person by their central characters.

The point of view and the revealed interior life belong to the central characters only.

Perhaps this partly explains their widespread success. The voices seemed new, contemporary and fresh, but the stories were very easy to read for those with little or no literary education and for people who were not interested in literature for its own sake but only in the support the stories gave to their solipsistic view of life. (Thus, Ian Hamilton requiring friends to read *Catcher* to see if they 'got it' as a test of their suitability for the bestowing of his favours.)

The Catcher in the Rye and *Bonjour Tristesse* are narratives that impressively maintain the first-person voices of their teenage protagonists. They are models of basic narrative structure and their authors' complete absorption in their characters' minds and feelings. They are admirable portraits of particular, singular individuals.

All stories of youth are inevitably stories of maturation. In this sense, both are novels about youth, and are useful as basic models of that kind of literature. But I wanted to do more in my novels, and in the telling of their stories, than these two did. I wanted them to include narrative strategies that Modernists such as Joyce, Lawrence, Woolf, Kafka, Hemingway, Mansfield, Proust, Stein, Duras, Beckett, B.S. Johnson, Vonnegut, Philip Roth, and others have developed. I go into some detail of my use of narrative strategies in the chapter 'Ways of Telling' and in the 'Interview' at the end of this book.

References
Ian Hamilton, *In Search of J.D. Salinger*, William Heinemann, 1988. Page 5.
Milan Kundera, *Writers at Work: The Paris Review Interviews*, Seventh Series, ed. George Plimpton, Secker & Warburg, 1987. Page 219.
Paul Ricoeur, *Oneself as Another*, trans. Kathleen Blamey, University of Chicago Press (1992), 1994. Page 151.
Françoise Sagan, *Bonjour Tristesse*, trans. Irene Ash, Penguin Books, 1958. Page 51.
J.D. Salinger, *The Catcher in the Rye*, Penguin Books, 1958. Pages 121, 179-80.
Viktor Shklovsky, *Theory of Prose*, trans. Benjamin Sher, Dalkey Archive Press (1990), 1991. Pages 62, 63.
Ludwig Wittgenstein, *Culture and Value*, ed. G.H. von Wright with Heikki Nyman, trans. Peter Winch, Basil Blackwell, 1980. Page 74e.

CHAPTER 4
HISTORY

When I began writing youth fiction in the 1960s it seemed an essential part of the job to find out if there was a history of such literature so that I could learn from it, become aware of the tradition, and then innovate from there.

Of course, I knew the long history of *bildungsroman*, exemplified by such seminal texts as Goethe's *Die Leiden des jungen Werthers* (*The Sufferings of Young Werther*), Charles Dickens' *Great Expectations*, and many others; stories which narrate the development of the protagonist from childhood to maturity. But these were not written with youth readers specifically in mind. What about fiction composed from that readerly perspective? For my limited purpose at that time, I inquired only into British and American examples. I want to pick out two threads that helped me.

The second thread was my reading of Mark Twain's *The Adventures of Huckleberry Finn*, which I'll come to in the next chapter. The first thread, considered here, is about what I learned from reading nineteenth-century stories, about English boys boarding in public (that is, private) schools, and about girls and their families in America.

I should emphasise that I'm not attempting an historical survey of youth fiction of the kind to be found, for example, in *Disturbing the Universe: Power and Repression in Adolescent Literature* by Roberta Seelinger Trites, and other scholarly sources. I'm only reporting reflections on how the two threads helped me when I began writing my own youth fiction and, in the case of *Huckleberry Finn*, still does.

A few years ago I was on a panel of writers at a conference on youth fiction. During question time a young man in the audience asked, 'When did writing for teenagers begin?' One of my fellow panellists gave the not uncommon answer, 'In the 1950s as part of the emergence of youth culture.'

I guess he had never heard of Sarah Trimmer.

From June 1802 until 1806 she published *The Guardian of Education* under the name 'Mrs Trimmer'. It was the first journal to review children's books seriously. In a manifesto article, 'Observations on the Changes Which have Taken Place in Books for Children and Young Persons', she declared that when discussing books for the young she would:

> ...endeavour to separate them into two distinct classes, viz. Books for Children, and Books for Young Persons; but where to draw the line may be the Question: formerly, all were reckoned Children, till they had at least attained their fourteenth year. Now, if we may judge from the titles of many little volumes, compared with their contents, we have Young Persons of five, or six years old. However, in our arrangement (assuming the privilege of authorship) we shall, without regard to title pages, take the liberty of adopting the idea of our forefathers, by supposing all young gentlemen and ladies to be Children, till they are fourteen, and young persons till they are at least twenty-one; and shall class the books we examine as they shall appear to us to be suitable to these different stages of human life.

Mrs Trimmer makes her distinction not on the grounds of literary form but on her assessment of moral suitability. She sees the need for a distinction, and understands that 'where to draw the line' is the problematic question. She also confirms the long-held belief that youthhood begins at about fourteen and goes on until at least twenty-one.

The fact is that by the time Jane Austen composed *North-*

anger Abbey, an innovative use of her adolescent popular reading, books intended for youth readers were already legion. In the next hundred years an honourable tradition was established of a literature which all through that time was uneasily accepted, if accepted at all, by the literary pundits.

BOYS AND SCHOOLS

Children's and youth fictions grew out of an intention to educate. School stories, or stories set in schools, abound in Britain from the late eighteenth century and are still being produced. I've written some myself. They are so numerous, they make up a separate category within youth literature.

It's not surprising that for most of that time, school stories were about boys. In those days girls of well-off families were mostly educated at home, if at all, or eventually – along with the rest of the population – at elementary neighbourhood schools. Boys of well-off families were sent to boarding school, often as early as eight but usually at thirteen, where they stayed until they were eighteen. Here was an eager and captive audience who lived for most of the year in an enclosed world that was a microcosm of the wider world. Apart from talk, books were the primary means of communication for both education and entertainment. Bringing the two together in fictions set in schools where the protagonists, the heroes and villains, were representative of the readers was an obvious move as soon as writers 'realised fully the importance of the adolescent, as distinct from the baby, stage in the younger generation', to use Harvey Darton's words in his magisterial study *Children's Books in England.*

It was in these stories that for the first time accounts of the living world were filtered through the particular and partial eyes of 'young persons'. These were stories in which controlling adults were often peripheral figures, who left the boys to get up to whatever mischief they could devise. A defining pleasure for their readers was the depiction of the goings-on of boys their own age when adults were out of sight and out of mind.

Perhaps the most famous example is *Tom Brown's Schooldays*, in which Tom is tortured over a fire by the bully Flashman, who is seventeen 'and big and strong for his age'. When the torture has gone so far that Tom faints, some of the boys intervene and send for the housekeeper. Flashman and his gang 'slink away'. The housekeeper administers first aid and Tom is taken to her room.

It's quite clear the boy is badly scorched on the back of his legs and that, as the housekeeper puts it, 'There's been some bad work here.' But none of the boys, Tom included, will 'peach' (tell the adults what has happened). To do so is to break a cardinal rule of schoolboy life; a rule respected, indeed encouraged, by the adult authorities as well as by the boys. So, 'Not a word could the housekeeper extract from [the boys]; and though the Doctor [headmaster] knew all that she knew that morning, he never knew more.' And he does nothing about it. The boys are left to deal with the matter themselves in their own way. The only comment by author-narrator Thomas Hughes is, 'I trust and believe that such scenes are not possible now at school.' Which is more than ingenuous. School stories, both factual and fictional published since *Tom Brown* appeared in 1857, provide plenty of evidence that Hughes's trust and belief were mistaken.

The school was based so closely on a real establishment, Rugby, where Hughes went as a boy, that alumni for years after testified to the accuracy of its setting and customs. This gave his story a reality never recorded so convincingly before. And he included events and behaviour previously thought inappropriate in fiction for the young. He took youths seriously and considered them worthy of telling the truth, even when it was unnerving.

It's true that in his portrait of the real headmaster Hughes seriously misrepresents Thomas Arnold, who was an educational innovator and father of the more famous Matthew. Also, it's true that, as Hughes confessed, his 'whole object in writing at all was to get a chance of preaching' to the young (quoted in Quigly). And yes, the image created, quite unintentionally I think, of an elite English 'public school' was extraordinarily influential and, to say the least, unfortunate. He promoted an ethos built not on academic study and a love of learning, but on sport and ruthless competition; an ethical aim summed up by the mantra 'country first, school next, self last'. It was a fictional image that was degraded to banality in the plethora of boarding school stories that *Tom Brown* spawned. And it became a lived-out reality that led to the fatal results of the First World War, demonstrating again how often life follows art rather than art following life.

Even so, Hughes did break new ground and pushed the boundaries of the school story. So did Talbot Baines Reed, even more innovatively. From his novels I learned, for example, that it's possible in a youth fiction to explore serious topics such as the practicalities of politics, as he does in *The Willoughby Captains*, and how an adult point of view can be narrated in such a way that it holds the interest of youth readers, as he does in *The Master of the Shell*, a novel about a young teacher in his first job, who admittedly is himself only just out of the age between.

The English boarding school story wasn't the only kind in which youth fiction had its evolution, but it was among the first to view everyday life through the eyes and perception of the youths who were the principal and plot-determining characters. However, the stories are told by an adult author-in-the-book who intervenes from time to time in his own voice. The tone is of youth being observed by grown-ups rather than of youth observing itself. And it's worth noting that none of the early school stories is written in the first-person voice of a youth protagonist, and none restricts itself only to a youthhood point of view.

GIRLS AND FAMILIES

In 1868, eleven years after Hughes published *Tom Brown* in England, Louisa May Alcott published *Little Women* in the US. What *Tom Brown* did for boys, *Little Women* did for girls, using the already familiar story of domestic family life as innovatively as Hughes used the school story. As Barbara Sicherman explains:

> Despite the use of John Bunyan's *Pilgrim's Progress* as a framing device, an older Calvinist worldview that emphasised sin and obedience to the deity has been replaced by a moral outlook in which self-discipline and doing good to others come first. Consonant with *Little Women*'s new moral tone, so congenial to an expanding middle class, are its informal style and rollicking escapades.

So far so true, but many others, such as Charlotte M. Yonge, Martha Finlay, Susan Coolidge, Ethel Turner, and Mrs Ewing did something of the same. The developments that helped make Alcott's book a classic were more technical in nature:

> She also had an ear for young people's language: her substitution of dialogue for the long passages of moralising narrative that characterised most girls' books gave her story a compelling sense of immediacy. So did her use of slang, for which critics often faulted her, but which must have endeared her to young readers.

This stylistic approach marks a shift from the adult-centred view of youth towards the view youths have of themselves. It's achieved mainly by attending to the language used by the young, and by composing the narrative so that it moves with youthful vigour and quickness.

As well as this, and as important, is Alcott's attention to character and the changing social and cultural attitudes to what girls could be and how they could behave. *Little Women*, like *Tom Brown's Schooldays*, was based not so much on invention or fantasy as on everyday reality. This gives the stories the appealing throb of actuality. 'The well-publicised autobiographical status of *Little Women*, together with Alcott's realistic subject matter and direct style, encouraged identification by middle-class readers,' Sicherman reports. She quotes testimonies of the book's influence on the lives of their youthful readers. The critic Cynthia Ozick, explaining how she became a writer, had written, for example: 'I read "Little Women" a thousand times' and 'I am no longer incognito, not even to myself. I am Jo in her "vortex"; not Jo exactly, but some Jo-of-the-future. I am under an enchantment: Who I truly am must be deferred, waited for and waited for.' Simone de Beauvoir 'caught a glimpse of my future self … I identified passionately with Jo, the intellectual … I became in my own eyes a character out of the novel.'

The influence was widespread. An impoverished child of Jewish immigrants living in a mid-western ghetto, Elizabeth G. Stern found *Little Women* among a stack of old newspapers in a rag shop. 'No book I have opened has meant as much to me as did that small volume telling in simple words such as I myself spoke, the story of an American childhood in New England … Often I think that I did not grow up in the ghetto but in the books I read as a child in the ghetto.'

In her eighties, speaking at her induction into the Connecticut Women's Hall of Fame, the African American writer Ann Petry related how *Little Women* was the first book she read on her own as a child. 'I couldn't stop reading because I had encountered Jo March. I felt as though I was part of Jo and she was part of me … She was a would-be writer – and so was I.'

PARACANONICAL TEXTS

Because she used to 'worship' *Little Women* when she was in third grade, 'a white, middle class, provincial girl, reciting entire chapters to myself' while she walked to school, Catharine R. Stimpson chose the book as an example of a 'paracanonical text' as distinct from the canon of texts established by time and elite authority as classics, whether one likes them or not. It's a useful distinction.

A paracanonical text is one that is enduringly popular, a novel 'some people have loved and do love', whether or not it is regarded by the academic and literary establishment as worthy to be accorded classic status, because it satisfies, in their authoritative opinion, the highest literary standards, and is therefore worthy of study and is a text which every educated reader should read.

Little Women has been paracanonical ever since it was first published. Now, it belongs both to a paracanon – it is still loved by many readers regardless of what any literary authority says about it – and it has become accepted by the academy as one of the few youth novels worthy of study.

Alcott valorised the everyday realities of adolescent life. For young readers she was on their side. She kept to a minimum the preaching of moral lessons and religious dogma, which was a predominant feature of stories for the young at that time. She didn't abandon the practice. But instead of making educational points herself, as a ubiquitous, grown-up narrator who knows better than the young characters, as Hughes did in *Tom Brown*, she allows characters in the story to do the work of thinking out the lessons to be drawn from events in the story. Her empathy has been rewarded by the passionate engagement of young readers with her novel.

Little Women is a novel about girls seen, inside and out, as the girls who read it saw themselves, either as they were or as they wanted to be, unfiltered through adult nostalgia. The characters are not observed but 'lived in'. For youth readers, the novel held the mirror up to their own nature. But it's still a story of girlhood narrated by a sympathetic adult. It isn't told by the young characters themselves. What

Alcott didn't do is make the move that eliminated the presence of the adult narrator entirely.

That author who did that was Mark Twain.

References

I've written extensively about Reed and his importance in 'Schools in Stories', in *Reading Talk*, Thimble Press, 2001.

Harvey Darton, *Children's Books in England: Five Centuries of Social Life*, third edition, Cambridge University Press, 1982. Page 285.

Thomas Hughes, *Tom Brown's Schooldays* (1857), Dent, 1949. Page 160.

Isabel Quigly, *The Heirs of Tom Brown*, Chatto and Windus, 1982. Page 53

Barbara Sicherman, 'Reading Little Women: The Many Lives of a Text', in Louisa M. Alcott, *Little Women or Meg, Jo, Beth and Amy*, ed. Anne K. Phillips & Gregory Eiselein, A Norton Critical Edition, W.W. Norton, 2004. Pages 644, 645, 634, 648, 651, 653.

Catharine R. Stimpson, 'Reading for Love: Canons, Paracanons and Whistling Jo March', in Alcott, *Little Women or Meg, Jo, Beth and Amy*, ed. Phillips & Eiselein, W.W. Norton, 2004. Page 584f.

Sarah Trimmer, 'The Guardian of Education', quoted from *A Peculiar Gift: Nineteenth Century Writings on Books for Children*, ed. Lance Salway, Kestrel Books, Penguin Books, 1976. Page 22.

Roberta Seelinger Trites, *Disturbing the Universe: Power and Repression in Adolescent Literature*, University of Iowa Press, 2000

CHAPTER 5
TWAIN AS HUCK

The Adventures of Huckleberry Finn stands out as not only a standard-setting and innovative development but as an instructive example of youth fiction. I've learned as much from it as from any other novel.

Critical theorists tell us the essential questions to ask of a narrative are:

Who tells? Who sees?

Who relates? Who focalises?

Who enacts? Who perceives?

So far in the history of stories deliberately intended for youth readers – *Tom Brown's Schooldays* and *Little Women* have been my examples – the one who tells is a mature adult, even when what is enacted, what is seen and known, are restricted to a focalising youth character. The stories have been told in the third person. And the adult narrator has in one way or another commented on the events and the characters either directly in the narrator's own voice or through the mouths of adult characters. Marmee, the mother in *Little Women*, explains the morality of the 'good way to live' to her children. Tom Brown's story is related and mediated quite openly by Thomas Hughes, *Little Women* by Louisa May Alcott's second self. The consciousness, the perception controlling the characters, their stories, the ethical aim, and the moral stance are an adult's consciousness.

Even when the interior, secret thoughts and emotions of the youth characters are revealed, they are inflected by the attitudes, beliefs and prejudices of the observing adult narrator. Unlike the cases of *The Catcher in the Rye* and *Bonjour Tristesse*, the reader is never in direct, unmediated contact with the young characters' consciousness.

The most obvious way to bring a youth character into direct contact with the reader is to make the person who sees and who tells, who enacts and who perceives, the central focalising character addressing us in his or her own first-person voice. Obvious though it seems now, after one hundred and fifty years of youth novels written in this voice, it was Mark Twain who first used it in *The Adventures of Huckleberry Finn* in 1884, fifty years or so after the emergence of books we can regard as youth fiction.

I don't mean to say that the work was an entirely new, unprecedented innovation. There was a library of stories told in the first-person voices of their protagonists. Twain had written some himself. But they were stories of adulthood. Their narrators were no longer youths themselves. With the exception of Goethe's *The Sufferings of Young Werther*, narrated in the first-person voice of the young protagonist, written when Goethe was twenty-four, and was therefore in the period of youthhood. Among other earlier first-person novels which depict young people, R. M. Ballantyne's *The Coral Island*, published in 1858, comes close but the first-person voice isn't completely that of the narrating youth. The narrating author's second self sometimes intrudes, glossing what the first-person narrator thinks or feels.

Huckleberry Finn is the first sustained, lengthy, substantial, utterly convincing first-person narration of a youth consciousness. Why did this evolution take so long? Was it because storybooks for children, out of which youth fiction grew, began as educational tools, used either for religious or social instruction? Writers were expected to guide their young readers in the paths of righteousness and good manners. They were required to be teachers who achieved their pedagogic aims by entertaining the reader.

Perhaps there was a fear among adults who controlled

what the young were allowed to read – parents, teachers, librarians, priests and ministers of religion, for example – that stories in which the young were given free rein to say in their own words what they thought and did out of sight, so to speak, of a regulating and mediating adult could lead to descriptions of misbehaviour and scandalous thoughts that might encourage young readers in similar goings-on.

Whatever the reasons, it was not until Twain created the character of Huck Finn that the first-person voice of youth entered the service of youth fiction in such a significant and permanently influential way that we can regard it as an innovative development.

Huck is not merely observed.

He is not described.

He is not recounted by an adult as a person of interest.

He is not used only as a figure in a plot.

Rather, he is subjectified.

He lives.

However, it's all very well saying Huck Finn's is an unmediated youthful consciousness; the fact remains that his story was written by a man in his forties, not by a boy in his youth. So we need to ask: How did Mark Twain become Huck Finn? Before answering that question I need to say something about 'becoming'.

To tell a story thoroughly in the first-person voice of a character, an author must so integrate with the character that all aspects of the telling are the character's own. Or, we might say, the author has to become the character so completely in his or her second self that everything seen, done, thought and said is related in the language of the character with such conviction that the reader accepts its reality.

Twain didn't become the full-bodied Huck of *The Adventures* from scratch. He came to him by way of the Huck who is a supporting player in *The Adventures of Tom Sawyer*, in which Huck is rather like Sancho Panza to Tom's Don Quixote. In the following paragraphs I rely on Victor A. Doyno's detailed study in *Writing Huck Finn: Mark Twain's Creative Process*. Because of Doyno's work on the drafts, letters, and other preparatory documents of Twain's novel, the kind of burgeoning scholarly study now called genetic criticism, we can follow in detail Twain's progress as he became Huck.

Tom Sawyer is written by an adult making use of his childhood memories to invent an adventure told in a wry tone of lightly satiric comedy tinged with nostalgia. When his editor, William Howells, read the manuscript he told Twain, 'It's altogether the best boy's story I ever read. It will be an immense success. But I think you ought to treat it explicitly as a boy's story.' The 'but' is suggestive. It can only mean Twain hadn't intended the book to be a story for boys. Twain replied, 'Mrs. Clemens decides with you that the book should issue as a book for boys, pure & simple – & so do I. It is surely the correct idea.'

We know Twain was never confident of the quality or even the nature of his work at the time of writing. He relied on Howells and on his wife, whose opinion was a force to be reckoned with. But later, after revising the story and reporting to Howells that he'd finished it, Twain made his own opinion plain. 'It's not a boy's book, at all. It will only be read by adults. It is only written for adults.'

The history of *Tom* proves he was wrong about boys not reading it. Perhaps he didn't allow for the fact that many young people are quite as capable of entering into the adult view of themselves as adults are of re-entering youthhood, if the fiction enables them to do so. But he was right about the narrator's tone of voice, and at times his direct address to an adult reader puts years between the storyteller and his young protagonists. A passage from the first chapter is an example. Tom has just been ticked off by Aunt Polly:

> Within two minutes, or even less, he had forgotten all his troubles. Not because his troubles were *one whit less*

> *heavy and bitter to him than a man's are to a man*, but because a new and powerful interest bore them down and drove them out of his mind for the time; *just as men's misfortunes are forgotten in the excitement of new enterprises.* This new interest was a valued novelty in whistling, which he had just acquired from a Negro, and he was suffering to practise it undisturbed. It consisted of a peculiar bird-like turn, a sort of liquid warble, produced by touching the tongue to the roof of the mouth at short intervals in the midst of the music. *The reader probably remembers how to do it if he has ever been a boy.*

I've italicised the phrases that indicate they are not a boy's thoughts, but those of the adult author. A boy cannot know from his own experience how heavy and bitter a man's troubles are to a man or that a man's misfortunes are forgotten by new excitements. At best, he could speculate, claiming to have witnessed the reactions of an adult at such times.

Twain's remark that *Tom* was not a book for boys comes in a reply to a letter from Howells in which Howells says of *Tom*, 'I really feel very much interested in your making that your chief work; you wont have such another chance; don't waste it on a boy.' Clearly, there had been discussion of *Tom* being only the beginning of an adult novel that followed the character into adulthood. But Twain says no.

> I have finished the story & didn't take the chap beyond boyhood. I believe it would be fatal to do it in any shape but autobiographically – like *Gil Blas*. I perhaps made a mistake in not writing it in the first person. If I went on, now, & took him into manhood, he would be just like all the one-horse men in literature & the reader would conceive a hearty contempt for him.

Alain-René Lesage's picaresque tale, *Gil Blas*, published in three volumes between 1715 and 1735, is about a resilient

Spanish youth, born in poverty of a stable hand and a chambermaid. He is educated by an uncle to such effect that aged seventeen he sets off for the University of Salamanca, only to be waylaid by robbers who force him to help them, which almost lands him in jail. Gil Blas becomes a valet, which brings him into contact with people of all classes and kinds, respectable and criminal, until by dint of his adaptability and quick wit he ends up rich and lives to tell the tale.

The parallels with *Huckleberry Finn* are obvious. Twain explains, 'By & by I shall take a boy of twelve & run him on through life (in the first person) but not Tom Sawyer – he would not be a good character for it.' A boy – not yet Huck Finn – telling his story in his own words, 'like Gil Blas'. That's the genesis of Huck. And the model for his story.

When did Twain decide 'a boy' should be Huck Finn?

It seems to have occurred sometime between Twain's letter to Howells dated July 5, 1875, and another a year later, dated August 9, 1876, in which he reports he has begun another boy's book. 'I have written 400 pages on it – therefore it is nearly half done. It is Huck Finn's Autobiography.'

He adds that he likes it 'only tolerably well' and 'may possibly pigeonhole or burn the manuscript when it is done.' Which rather suggests he hasn't yet fully entered into Huck or thought of him as the boy of the book he told Howells he wanted to write, which followed a boy through to manhood.

By the way, 400 pages written in a month might seem copious. But Twain handwrote spaciously on pages less than A5 in size, with around 100 words a page. A rough reckoning suggests he'd written about 40,000 words, averaging about 1,500 a day, which for Twain, a fecund and fluent writer when in full flow, was moderate rather than torrential.

What seems to have happened next is that Twain worked at the book in two periods, 1879 or 1880 and 1883 to 1884. By May 1883 the manuscript was about 50,000 words. He finished with about 70,000, and revised intensively and in great detail. He wrote to Howells on July 20, 1883:

> I haven't piled up MS so in years as I have done since we came here to the farm three weeks & a half ago ... I wrote 4000 words to-day and I touch 3000 & upwards pretty often, & don't fall below 2600 on any working day. And when I get fagged out, I lie abed a couple of days & read and smoke, & then go at it again for 6 or 7 days.

I won't follow in detail the writing process any further. I only want to make it clear that the creation of *Huck Finn* was a slow and groping process, until Twain entered into the story wholeheartedly, when it flowed out of him full pelt. For example, at the top of the first page of the manuscript that eventually became his greatest book, Twain wrote:

> Huckleberry Finn
> Reported by
> Mark Twain

Not just Huck, but Huckleberry, as if to indicate that this Huck is of a different status and is a more complete being than the Huck of *Tom Sawyer*. And his story is 'reported', not invented by Twain.

Doyno's investigation shows what pains Twain took to make sure Huck's voice is his own and no one else's. He revised meticulously. Doyno demonstrates with numerous examples how:

> All the revisions in the novel are, in a way, revisions of Huck's voice, with the possible exception of changes in other characters' speech (although purists could theoretically argue that even these changes are examples of Huck's scrupulous retelling, in dialect, of his experiences). The revisions of other voices permit little doubt about the precision of Twain's artistry.

In other words, all the changes were made so that every detail in the story is recorded as it would be by Huck himself, even when the changes are to the direct speech of other characters. What other characters say is expressed in Huck's version of what he heard; this does not mean it is precisely what the characters actually said and how they said it, just as when we relate incidents in our own lives they are our remembered versions of what was said and done, which everyone understands may not be a precisely accurate record. The entire story is filtered through Huck's consciousness and related within the limits of his maturity, the nature of his personality, his experiences of life, and his way of telling.

We see Twain doing this right from the beginning. The first words of the first draft of the first sentence were:

'You will not know about the...'

This was changed in the second draft to:

'You do not know about me...'

And changed again in the third and final draft to:

'You don't know about me...'

This may seem trivial. But that's the point. It's an example of the care Twain took in creating Huck's diction.

Twain pays the same attention to Huck's perception; his view of people and their actions, conditioned by his early youthhood and (im)maturity. The most obvious example deals with Huck's often-remarked sexual naivety. It's a passage in which Huck tells us his opinion of Miss Mary Jane Wilks, the older adolescent girl whose inheritance is almost stolen by the fraudulent King and Duke. Huck admires her pluck. The first draft has him saying, 'there warn't no backdown to her, if I know a girl by the rake of her stern; and I think I do,' adding that 'I hain't never seen her since that time I see her go out at the door, and turn at the stairs and kinder throw a kiss back at me'.

Twain deleted both.

Knowing a girl by the rake of her stern is too crassly adult.

And the kiss thrown back is too flirtatious on the part of the direct and forthright Mary Jane, who doesn't behave like that in any other scene, and again, is too sexually knowing of Huck, who is reporting the event and would therefore see it in his own light. Even if Mary Jane had blown the kiss, Huck would not have perceived it as other than affectionately playful and not necessarily as Mary Jane intended it.

None of this is explicit. The implications are carried in the choice of word and image: 'the rake of her stern' is the language and image of a boastful experienced man; 'throw a kiss back at me' is an intimate gesture, suggesting a closer relationship than Huck had with the girl. And the ambiguous 'back at' suggests that Huck had thrown one to Mary Jane first.

Twain applies this focalising rigour to every aspect of the story: to Huck's moralising, his tussle with the subtleties of what it is right to do and what it is wrong to do, his thoughts about religion, his growing understanding of loyalty and friendship, truth and falsehood, authority and freedom, his judgements of people, his descriptions of the natural world, his own duplicity, his obstinate determination to do what seems best, for good or ill, for himself, and for those he comes to admire – as he does the escaped slave Jim, the relationship which brings to a climax the ethical aim of the story, when Huck has to decide whether to give Jim up as the law and Huck's own safety require, or not to and risk the dire consequences his decision could entail.

Huck learns, scene by scene, the awkward adjustments of life that youthhood brings to a boy's consciousness, and we observe him as he learns them.

If there is a moment when youth literature is born as an art form as well as an entertainment, rather than as an educational vehicle for conventionally approved social, religious, moral or instructional teaching, it is the publication of Mark Twain's *Adventures of Huckleberry Finn* first in Britain in December 1884, and then in the US in February 1885. To clear away an opposing opinion, it could be claimed that Robert Louis Stevenson's *Treasure Island* (and not *Huckleberry Finn*) was the first masterpiece of an adolescent boy's first-person narrative. It appeared as a serial in the children's magazine *Young Folks* between 1881 and 1882 before publication as a book on 23 May 1883: that is, eighteen months before Twain's work. It's remarkable that both authors, presumably unknown to each other, were writing at the same time books which are evolutionary landmarks in the history of our literature.

Both stories bring into play ethical and moral questions which until then had not been treated, if at all, unless confined within didactic restrictions on what was regarded as suitable for the young to read. Both stories dramatically confront conflicts of truth and deceit, loyalty and betrayal, justice and mercy, society's conventional moral codes and personal freedom. Both stories are fully achieved first-person narratives in the voices of their protagonists.

Why, then, privilege *Huckleberry Finn* over *Treasure Island*? For at least two reasons.

First, *Treasure Island* is constrained by being an adventure story rather than anything else, set a hundred years or so before the time of writing, and driven by its plot rather than by an interest in the interior life of its characters. *Huck*, though thoroughly plotted, is concerned not with the events themselves as the reason for telling the story but with the behaviour of Huck and the other characters, their motives and personalities and how they work out the circumstances and dilemmas of their lives, as these are understood by Huck. The story takes place in the lifetime of the author; it is a contemporary and realistic fiction, not an historical one. The story and the telling are enriched by an interest in the nature of human beings. I'd say, this is the main point of the story. The search for the treasure and the adventures on the way to finding it are the main interest of *Treasure Island*. Jim happens to be the storyteller. Huck himself is the main interest and focus of *Huckleberry Finn*.

Second reason: the person of the narrator.

How old is Jim Hawkins when the story happens, and how old is he when he tells it? How old is Huck when his story happens and when he tells it?

At the end of *Treasure Island* Jim relates what's happened to some of the main characters since they got back to England. Among them is the sailor called Gray, who 'studied his profession; and he is now mate and part owner of a fine full-rigged ship; married besides, and the father of a family'. It must have taken quite a few years after the events in the book for Gray to do all that.

We're not told how old Jim is. But in the main narrative he's of an age to be taken on as a cabin boy. In the eighteenth century, cabin boys were often as young as eleven and not much older than fourteen. That sounds about right for Jim, to judge by his behaviour and the way he is treated in the story by the adult characters.

Given the time Gray takes to become a qualified mate, part owner of a large ship, and a married man with a family, Jim must be at least in his late thirties when he writes the story. This means he is an adult looking back to a time when he was a boy. He makes no pretence of telling the story as if in its immediate present. His narration incorporates his adult re-view of himself as a pubescent or early adolescent boy. He is not relating the story as it happened, or immediately afterwards, but as he remembers it. This distances him from himself as he was at the time, and he doesn't pretend otherwise. He doesn't become his young self.

How old is Huck at the beginning of his story? Twelve, if we go by Twain's letters. And by the book? Fifteen or sixteen.

We know this because he tells us that Aunt Sally wants to adopt him and 'sivilize' him. In order to avoid that awful fate he is going to escape to the 'Territory' – the untamed West. In other words, he isn't old enough to be legally independent. But old enough to get by on his own. Which means he tells his story while still close to the time of its events and while he is still in his youthful consciousness.

Huckleberry Finn is a novel that more precisely and extensively than *Treasure Island* is a work of immanent youth and is therefore more useful as a paradigm of youth fiction. And for me this makes *Huck* a truly literary novel, whereas *Treasure Island* is a romanticised historical adventure that incorporates features of the literary novel – considerations of life – without these being the story's primary purpose.

I don't mean to denigrate or minimise the achievement of *Treasure Island*. I first read it and *Huck* when I was in my early teens and loved both. I enjoyed it for its page-turning power as an adventure story. It was not until I was an adult studying children's books as literature and as an author setting out to write youth fiction that I noticed its treatment of moral and ethical aspects of human life. Whereas I enjoyed *Huck* because it was about human beings and the way they behave, Huck himself most of all. It was full of incidents of a much greater variety than those in *Treasure Island*, but it was the characters who held my interest. *Huck* was a book that made me think about life, and that's why I read it more than once. I knew once was not enough.

Both books are called 'Adventures'. Both are. But one is the adventure of eventful action set in a fantasised, romanticised time and place. The other is the adventure of a growing mind, a developing personality, set in an actual place, and in a time contemporary with its narrator as well as its author.

I've spent so much space on the creation of *Huckleberry Finn* and how it was achieved not only because of its importance in the history of youth literature, but because for me it's a model of what youth fiction can be, and how it is created as literature in its own right, distinctly different from the literature of childhood and the literature of adulthood.

References

I've explored other aspects of *Huckleberry Finn* in my essay, 'All of a Tremble to See His Danger' in *Reading Talk*, Thimble Press, 2001.

Victor A. Doyno, *Writing Huck Finn: Mark Twain's Creative Process*, University of Pennsylvania Press (1991), 1993. Pages 19, 22, 23, 46.

Ron Powers, *Mark Twain: A Life*, Free Press, Simon & Schuster, 2005. Page 379.

Robert Louis Stevenson, *Treasure Island* (1882), Oxford University Press, 2011. Page 182.

Mark Twain, *Adventures of Huckleberry Finn* (1884), ed. Thomas Cooley, Norton Critical Edition, Third Edition, W.W. Norton, 1999. Page 10-11.

Mark Twain, *The Adventures of Tom Sawyer* (1876), Puffin Books, 1950. Page 10-11.

DEFINING YOUTH AND YOUTH LITERATURE

CHAPTER 6
MARKS OF YOUTH

Because I believe youth fiction to be literature with a poetics of its own – a literature which is primarily determined by the consciousness of youthhood, and mainly occupied by the experience of living through the age between – a study of the nature of youthhood is necessary. I first set this out in *The Reluctant Reader* in 1969. What follows is an updated version of that analysis, which takes account of the considerable knowledge neuroscientists, and especially brain scientists, have provided in recent years.

The sources I've found most helpful are the books by Maryanne Wolf, listed in the references. For twenty-five years Wolf has studied the science of what happens in the brain as we read. This and other aspects of life in youthhood are conveniently reported in everyday language by David Bainbridge in *Teenagers: A Natural History*, to which I acknowledge my debt in this chapter.

LANGUAGE

This we accept: Human beings are a language-using and storytelling animal. We inherit our biological condition from our genes. We learn our cultural life from memes. That is, by imitating those who from birth care for us, and later those who we admire, and to whom we want to belong.

As Bainbridge reminds us, 'Most of what we get from others comes in the form of language'. We have a 'non-genetic, non-behavioural means of conveying information'. By using language, we 'warn, advise, charm, threaten and inform'. We tell stories about where we come from, who we belong to, how life used to be, how it is now, and how it could be. And we can imagine that which does not yet exist and which we are then able to create.

Most of our skills with language, along with some of our ability to interpret meaning, are acquired by the age of ten. The language centres in the human brain are located in the prefrontal cortex. They specialise in creating and interpreting speech.

It is in childhood that acquisition of language mostly occurs but, Bainbridge reports, this is 'fundamentally different to adolescent cognitive development.' How is it different? Teenagers, he says, 'are connecting their language systems to the formidable cognitive armoury developing in their frontal lobes.' Their thinking is more complex than in childhood, and they discover subtleties of nuance, sarcasm, irony and satire. They learn how to consciously manipulate others, the difference between affection and malice. They test the boundaries of acceptable and unacceptable behaviour. 'And of course flirting is the most delightfully elaborate form of teenage communication, one in which all the post-childhood skills are brought to bear – humour, teasing, tone, style and astonishing feats of circumlocution.'

We all remember this. That there is now scientific evidence showing how it comes about helps us understand why teenagers can be difficult, annoying, and often upsetting.

But there is more to it than this; a mark of youth that is frequently misunderstood and even causes distress. Teenagers tend to talk more and more with their peers rather than with their parents or other responsible adults. And they develop language and other forms of communication particular to the different social groups to which they belong. One kind is acceptable for use with adults. Another kind is slang, argot, jokes, codes, accents that connect and bind them to their preferred peer groups; language which many adults find incomprehensible, and when they do understand often find annoying or unacceptable. Teenagers switch easily from one to another, from the conventionally respectable to the modishly inventive, humorous, often rebellious and disrespectful. Which is why they love vulgar anarchic comedy, satire, and anything that makes fun of adults and debunks socially acceptable behaviour.

They test the boundaries of language just as they test the boundaries of behaviour. They like to see how far they can go before everything breaks down.

Youth fiction, if it is to be the literature of youthness, must incorporate and depict adolescent experience and use of language as it evolves in their private, secret, interior selves, as well as in their social lives. This is fundamental to the poetics of the form. J. D. Salinger's *The Catcher in the Rye* provides a clear example.

But here's the rub. Using contemporary argot will quickly date a story. For example, Holden's language was audacious in the 1950s. Now it's quaintly old-fashioned, not radical and audacious at all. *Catcher* is a model that many writers have adopted in their attempts to write for, and be commercially successful with, a large youth readership. As a result, their work is ephemeral, because after a short time it's no longer of immediate interest to the readership for which it was deliberately intended, a readership that wants the instant satisfaction of stories that are about themselves now, using their peer-group language, their fashions, their ways of thought and behaviour. Language and fashions that change rapidly.

How to achieve the voice of a youth narrator and the dialogue of youth characters, which remain convincing over the years without becoming dated, is one of the challenges facing authors of youth literature.

One solution I've tried is to avoid current slang by inventing my own or using now-forgotten language from years ago which has the sound of slang, a meaning easily understood in context, and gives the impression that the characters are linguistically inventive and witty. (Again, the rule applies about getting the balance right between over- or underuse of the slang.) Another solution is to compose a conversational style based on usage at the time the story takes place, without employing the slang current at that time. Robert Cormier does this in *The Chocolate War*, published in 1974.

Nowadays, another linguistic development has evolved which complicates the depiction of youth. In recent years young people have added new electronic and digital means of communication to their repertoire. A new vocabulary, new styles, new forms of narrative of actual or fictional events are being created. These are growing and changing so fast that a list of those currently fashionable would be completely out of date before this book is published.

For example I have in front of me, pulled from the internet, a list of 396 'acronyms and shorthand' described as 'an integral part of computer culture'. They range from the obvious '2B or not 2B' to the clueless 'YYSSW': 'Yeah Yeah Sure Sure Whatever'. And no doubt the list grows longer day by day. Does anyone, even the most nerdish youth, know and use all 396? Or does the list, like the dictionary, contain many now rarely or never used and some already archaic, wholly known in total only by the digital communication equivalent of lexicographers? This is a small example of how quickly the language of communication is elaborating its own spelling, punctuation, grammar, diction, and ethics. Any story written in the consciousness of those aged fourteen to twenty-five and set in contemporary times is bound to incorporate this linguistic cultural development, and this newly essential feature of youthness.

No plot would be convincing at present if mobile phones, voice, text and other digital messaging were not used, unless authors could devise ingenious, plot-significant reasons for characters not to use them.

I read that neuroscientists are finding evidence that the

adolescent brain is rapidly evolving to make it possible for numerous mental activities to be processed simultaneously. Talking, texting, surfing the web, listening to music, and doing homework all at the same time are usual now, sometimes to the worried puzzlement of parents.

These developments have another consequence. Because they make such complicated demands, it is taking the brain longer to mature. Which explains why the period of youth seems to be getting longer, extending beyond the teenage years well into the twenties. This is one reason for the increase in the school leaving age and the continuation of formal education into what used to be thought young adulthood. The brain simply needs more time to reach maturity.

SELF-AWARENESS

The troublesome bodily changes during youthhood are accompanied by a surge in self-awareness: the growing knowledge of oneself. Children become self-conscious of course, more and more as the years pass. But their perception of themselves is patchy; it is not as persistent and probing, nor as all-consuming, as it becomes during youthhood.

Everyone knows from experience how unremitting and painful this self-conscious analysis can be. Hours are often spent poring over every smallest detail of your being, from the agonising dissatisfaction with your physical appearance to the puzzling questions of what you are, who you are, what you believe, what you will become, and what other people think of you. Most of us are more self-critical during our youth than we ever are again. But we are also more vulnerable to criticism by others, especially our peers – the youths who are our closest friends and those groups to which we want to belong – and by adults with authority over us, such as parents, relatives, teachers, and the police.

It is self-analysis that facilitates human beings' unrivalled mental flexibility. And it's during youthhood that we consciously discover this and practice using it. We learn how to solve problems beyond the capacity of children, how to rethink something we cannot do and find a way to succeed.

A lot of what happens during the age between is experienced consciously for the first time: for example, falling in love, managing your sexuality, earning and spending your own money, being responsible for yourself, such as when travelling alone, negotiating with others to achieve your self-chosen goals. Because in this period of life we are green in experience we often make mistakes and sometimes behave aggressively when we are thwarted or opposed. We are still learning how to cope with the roil of unrefined emotions that conflict us. Youth fiction is bound to narrate this universal experience.

DE-IDENTIFICATION AND AUTONOMY

One of the ways I think about the difference between childhood and youthhood is this:

Childhood is the condition in which we believe we are what adults tell us we are, and behave as they want us to behave. Or, to quote Wordsworth's 'Ode: Intimations of Immortality', it is 'As if his whole vocation/Were endless imitation'.

Youthhood is the condition in which we question whether we are, or want to be, what we have been told we are and have been pretending to be. It's a time when we strive to become self-determining and independent. Some scientists go so far as to suggest that we undergo, as Bainbridge puts it, 'a complete internal restructuring of the mind's view of itself.'

In other words, in our youth we seek autonomy. To achieve this requires self-analysis. But you can't achieve autonomy if you remain under the sway of the people who authored you, and have the power of authority over you.

The answer to this existential dilemma is de-identification. You have to establish your own identity by unhitching yourself from parents, relatives, legal guardians and carers.

Inevitably, this generates conflicts. In youth we challenge our controlling adults; their opinions, beliefs, lifestyles, rules, expectations of us. We seek to be free of their control, exclude them from our new life-choices, both social and personal. And yet at the same time we expect them to continue to support us practically and emotionally despite our rebelliousness, and cut up rough if they don't give it. This is the cause of the familiar accusation that adolescents are selfish, egotistic, emotionally volatile, rude, offensive, self-defensive, aggressive, opinionated, and thoughtless. Just for starters.

But we learn from the experience of this turmoil. We become conscious of self-interest and altruism; selfishness and self-sacrifice; self-confidence and vulnerability; emotional demands we make on others and emotional demands others make on us; attachments wrought by falling in love and the distress, the pain, of rejection and falling out of love; the flux of secrecy and declaration and the dangers of both; the power and tactics of manipulation and the oppression of being manipulated; our spiritual and moral, political and social beliefs; and much more.

Oscar Wilde says that experience is the name we give our mistakes. And it is a truism that youthhood is a time of constant experiment, which is abundant in mistakes. We learn more by trial and error in the age between than at any other time of life. It's a bumpy ride to maturity with many breakdowns on the way. We witness this played out on stage in *Romeo and Juliet*, narrated in novels like *Huckleberry Finn*, Raymond Radiguet's *The Devil in the Flesh* and *Bonjour Tristesse*, and we are moved by its daily progress, as poignantly recorded in *The Diary of Anne Frank*.

Youthhood is the liveliest school of life. Never such bright shining morning again.

WORRY, ANXIETY, SADNESS

Turmoil causes worry. The simultaneous onset of life-changing developments we do not seem able to control, and for which we are not responsible, causes anxiety. (When will they end? What are they doing to my body, mind and soul? What will other people think of me because of them?) Worry caused by turmoil is understandable. Anxiety caused by eruptions in your body and disruptions in your home and social life is inevitable. Not surprising, then, that we suffer extreme mood swings from high to low, from pleasurable to distressing. T.S. Eliot says human beings cannot bear very much reality. But neither can we bear very much confusion.

Living through adolescence is a balancing act. From time to time we make mistakes and fall. When we fall we feel we have failed. A succession of failures makes us feel sad. When sadness persists for more than a few days we can slide into depression. Depression feels like being trapped in a deep dark hole from which there is no escape.

Bouts of sadness, from feeling low for a day or two to serious long-lasting depression, are so usual in this stage of life that they used to be dismissed as 'growing pains'. But there is more to it than that. A distinguishing mark of adolescence is what Bainbridge calls 'teenage sadness'. But he doesn't mean a mundane condition. He means something more fundamental, even elemental. A sadness so particular to adolescence that it 'warrants a new category' – an evolutionary development which could not be known about until recent advances in the brain sciences.

A pointer. Between one third and one half of teenagers in the US report being 'sad' or 'in turmoil' at any one time. This is an extraordinary percentage compared with the rest of the population. Bainbridge suggests it 'indicates that something changes dramatically in the second decade of life.' Something so distinctly different and so profound that:

> Whether it can be blamed on the extensive anatomical restructuring of the teenage brain, or more 'psychiatric' concepts such as the development of self-analysis and

the quest for autonomy, it seems clear that teenage mood alters because the teenage brain alters. And if the teenage brain is supposed to change, should we not expect teenage sadness to occur?

If Bainbridge is right, and there is increasing research evidence that he is, authors of youth fiction need to take this into account, and, along with those who study the literature, need to pay attention to the growing body of evocriticism, a rapidly emerging field of literary study that considers from an interdisciplinary point of view the relationship that human beings have with the environment and applies knowledge of the adaptive behaviour of human beings to a reading of fiction.

COMPETITIVENESS

During my time as a student teacher in the mid-1950s I was encouraged to conduct a sociometric study of a class of fourteen-year-old boys with the aim of understanding the social relationships in the class. The boys filled in a simple questionnaire, answering questions such as 'Which boy do you like best?', 'Which boy do you dislike most?', 'Who do you admire most?', 'Who do you admire least?'

I started out sceptical and was surprised by the clarity of the result. There were two main groups (gangs), each dominated (led) by the most admired and liked boy. He was the 'star'. One or two boys were accepted by each group because they had a friend in the other group. Otherwise membership of each group was exclusive and rivalrous. The two leaders were friendly and admired each other but they were competitive, each setting his group against the other when desired.

There were two other small groups. One group, called 'rejects' by the sociometric designers, had been thrown out of the dominant groups usually because, for one reason or another, they weren't liked by the members or because they had committed some 'sin'. These boys tended to hang about together, eyeing the dominant groups with resentment or longing, and sometimes tried to ingratiate themselves back inside by sucking up to the leaders. It rarely worked. They were made use of and then rejected again.

The other even smaller group was of boys called 'isolates'. They didn't want to belong to any group. Though identified as a group in the diagrammatic design of the study, they had very little to do with each other. They preferred to be on their own and keep to themselves.

The thing they had in common was that they were unconcerned by anything said about them by the groupies. They weren't subdued by gibes and insults nor seduced by praise and approval. In fact, they were strong-willed, usually brighter than most, rather admired for their independence and often on good terms with the 'stars', who would sometimes chat them up and pick their brains. They were true loners.

As a research method this was crude. But it was indicative. Youths, like all human beings, are herd animals. They need to be together, to belong to groups of other people they admire and want to be like, groups which provide security, social and practical support and an identity. And they are hierarchic. They need leaders and a social structure they can understand.

Hierarchies impel competitiveness. There is a pecking order. You compete, whether you are conscious of doing so or not, to be approved of by those with power and influence, and to rise in the structure, or to have influence with the leaders and with the rest of the group. You will sometimes override your personal preferences and even your moral and ethical standards in order to remain in the group, be accepted by it, and be of some account in it.

This is cultural. The cultural replicators are memes – ideas – which are transmitted by those with power, influence and authority who are admired and imitated by many. In other words, cultural behaviour is learned by copying.

Robert Cormier's youth novel *The Chocolate War* provides an exemplar of this happening among a group of teenage pupils in a school. Jerry Renault becomes a 'reject' because of his opposition to the leader's demands, is then manipulated to increase the leader's power and influence, and all but dies for the stand he takes. Jerry's actions reveal the mendacity and moral weaknesses of the other boys, who do whatever is necessary to stay in the leader's good books and to keep their place in the group.

Another example is the moral crisis at the heart of *Huckleberry Finn*: the scene in which Huck has to decide whether or not to give up Jim, the runaway slave, to the authorities. By doing so he will be accepted and approved of by the leaders of the hierarchically controlled group we call 'society'. By not doing so he knows he will be punished, perhaps even killed, for behaviour that is both socially unacceptable and unlawful. His only way of avoiding this fate is to escape to the untamed, still lawless Wild West in order to be true to himself. He becomes an 'isolate', a loner, rather than submit to a group, whose hypocritical mores he has seen through.

In *Catcher*, Holden behaves like an isolate, but in fact he wants to belong to a group of which he is the protecting leader. Another of the books written by a teenager, S.E. Hinton's youth novel *The Outsiders*, is a depiction of the dynamics of gangs during youthhood. A earlier novel, a model of what can be done, is *The Confusions of Young Törless* by Robert Musil, published as an adult book in 1906.

SEX AND LOVE

It is a hoary joke that seventy per cent of teenagers' waking lives is spent thinking about sex. Whatever the actual percentage there's no doubting the truth of the suggestion. From the onset of pubescence sex is a constant preoccupation. The consuming desire for it, the vivid fantasies about it, the puzzling techniques of it, the disabling worries about attractiveness, the restraining fear of humiliation if rejected, the anxieties about contraception, sexually transmitted diseases and, for girls, the fear of getting pregnant.

Much is learned by trial and error and, these days, from easily accessed internet pornography, which helps teenagers to be a great deal better informed than used to be the case but which doesn't necessarily make them any the wiser. Generally speaking, in Britain and America and in other parts of the world too, sex education in schools is woefully inadequate. Age-old moral, ethical, religious and cultural taboos prevent teachers providing information about some aspects of sex, never mind discussion of them. Least explored of all are the emotional and psychological entanglements of this elemental experience of human life. Information without context, without some imaginal understanding of the felt realities, is not only useless but can be dangerous.

If you believe, as I do, that literature is peculiarly valuable because (as Richard Hoggart summarised) 'it explores, re-creates and seeks for meanings in human experience; because it explores the diversity, complexity and strangeness of that experience ... because it re-creates the texture of that experience', it follows that youth literature must explore all the experiences of youth. To rule out sex, as was usual in the past, is to misrepresent the actuality. Simply stated, it's impossible to depict the whole of youthhood without narrating the part sex plays in the age between. Fiction is the thought experiment that helps us deal with it, especially the emotional and psychological aspects of it.

Sex is much more explicitly included in youth fiction these days than it used to be. The question is not whether sex should be included but how it's narrated. How much should be told and how explicitly? And why? What is its purpose in this story, this scene? Why is it necessary other than as an arbitrary description of the sex act? I'm not saying that sex has to be included in every youth fiction. It doesn't have a place in every story, any more than it has a place in every human encounter, except perhaps for those who are pathologically over-sexed.

Let me offer my own attempts as an example. To start with, I'm guided by a rule I apply to all of youth literature. What can be told is only that which the consciousness of the focalising character can know in real life, intelligently perceive, actively learn or observe in the lives of other people.

I explain in detail in the chapter 'Ways of Telling' how I intended *Breaktime* to be a novel that deals in the physical aspects of life: the experience of the five senses and the resulting emotional and mental responses. Ditto, the seventeen-year-old central character and narrator, is very aware of his body, what happens to it and how it feels. And he longs to have his first sexual experience with a girl. When it happens, he narrates it in three ways which are meant to be understood as simultaneous experience.

His description is explicit. But when read together, the combined effect of the three parallel passages prevents the reader from focusing only on the sex act. Instead, the scene becomes comic. However, implicit in Ditto's story, which he has written for his friend Morgan, the implied reader, is the question whether or not this is a factual account of a real-life encounter or a story he has invented, a sexual fantasy.

That question indicates the ethical aim, not only of the sex scene but of the whole novel. Ditto sets out to have sex for the first time. His experience of achieving it, whether actual or imagined, makes clear to him that sex for physical pleasure only is not sufficient for what Paul Ricoeur calls 'an accomplished life'. During postcoital sleep his one-night partner, Helen, slips away, leaving a note which thanks him for being a 'help', saying she doubts they will meet again, and ending with the valediction 'Be loved'. Two words which sum up what Ditto has learned. Sex might be 'a help' but on its own it is ephemeral. It is not 'love'. In more than one sense it leaves a lot to be desired.

Dance on My Grave, the second in a six-book sequence, begins where *Breaktime* left off, with the focalising narrator's desire to be loved. Sixteen-year-old Hal falls for eighteen-year-old Barry, who he thinks has fallen for him. Hal finds out, with a little help from his friend Kari, a young Norwegian woman, that what he felt for Barry was not the kind of love he had thought it was, and the kind he wanted. In my words, not Hal's, in the context of this story there are two kinds of love: immature love and mature love.

Immature love occurs, as it frequently does during adolescence, when we believe we have found the ideal lover, the one we have longed for. Whereas what we have done is project that fantasy onto the other person. We are infatuated. Sooner or later we learn the hard way that the other person is not who or what we imagined, and what we wished they were. And we fall out of love – out of infatuation – with considerable distress and often with embarrassment and anger directed at ourselves. It is a chastening education.

Mature love occurs when we fall in love with the other person because of who and what they are, warts and all. We are aware of their reality, of their strengths and weaknesses, their good points and their bad. Even then, of course, we can be mistaken. Repellent characteristics which have been hidden can rise to the surface, take us by surprise and lead to disaffection. Nothing in life is certain; there are no absolutes; but we wish there were and seek them all our lives. But that is a story that lies in wait for the four novels that follow *Dance on My Grave*.

Ditto and Hal confuse the difference between sex and love, between the wished-for and the actual. Quite often during the age between, nothing seems more important, more complicated or more difficult to untangle. Stories can help them understand their confusions.

There are other forms of love besides sexual and romantic: the love of family, for example, of friendship, of dedicated work, of ideas, of what people often call God, of language, music, art, and science, and the love of nature.

Bainbridge and Maryanne Wolf supply in everyday language the biological information and especially the neuroscience that helps us understand what happens during youth, showing how it is not a modern cultural development, as is sometimes claimed, but 'a biological phenomenon unique in the animal kingdom'. Bainbridge calls it 'a constellation of carefully timed events' during which, as is frequently observed, girls develop faster than boys – hence girls' frequent preference of older boys and young men, and their dismissal of same-aged boys as puerile, immature and silly. Youth literature narrates the drama of this complex maturation.

JOY, EPIPHANY, THE APORIAS OF THE SOUL, AND SPIRITUALITY

An editor I worked with in the 1970s used to say that all 'teenage fiction' could be given the same title: Misunderstood. Her remark reflected her dislike of what she regarded as a spurious category, but there is some truth in it. To judge by many youth novels, their young characters never experience times of joy, exuberance, unsullied pleasure, or awe and delight, that are as much part of youthhood as the travails, pains, anxieties and sadness endured during the age between.

Unhappiness is easier to describe than happiness and is usually more dramatic. But if literature is to encompass all of life, it must include those times when, as Ben Jonson expressed it, 'in short measures life may perfect be.' During most people's adolescence these are not in short supply.

One of those 'short measures' is the experience of epiphany; a moment of 'showing forth', a sudden almost overwhelming revelation to do with yourself, the world, and life itself. And as it happens, such moments occur most frequently and most intensely during our youth.

I've always tried to relate the 'short measures' in my youth fictions. When I was preparing to write *Now I Know*, in which I knew the central character, seventeen-year-old Nik, would experience an epiphany, I came across real-life episodes of this kind written by youths, which helped me describe it. They were included in Michael Paffard's book *Inglorious Wordsworths*, the result of Paffard's research in the 1970s, which he subtitled 'A study of some transcendental experiences in childhood and adolescence'. It includes extracts from many accounts written by pupils aged sixteen to eighteen and university students of nineteen and twenty years old. 'It seems likely,' Paffard writes, 'that future historians looking back at the twentieth century will observe that we have generally been as reticent about the spirit or soul as the nineteenth century was about sex.'

Like the fiction written by youths themselves, the autobiographical episodes Paffard quotes are first-hand evidence. He explains in detail the background to his project, the reason for it, the process, and his analyses of the results. A questionnaire he devised was completed by 475 respondents. In one chapter he groups the answers into 'a variety of experiences':

1 **Joy:** Rapture, ecstasy, including experiences of exceptional and unadulterated happiness.
2 **Pleasure:** happiness; agreeable and desirable feelings not reaching the intensity of joy.
3 **Enchantment:** heightened awareness of perception; sudden and exceptional feelings of mental, physical or moral well-being.
4 **Calm:** peace, satisfaction, relief, contentment.
5 **Trance:** withdrawal experiences including sense of loss of time, place, or personal identity; unitive experiences, merging with surroundings, etc.
6 **Longing:** yearning, desire.
7 **Melancholy:** sadness, desolation, loneliness.
8 **Awe:** humility, sense of smallness, of being overwhelmed, overpowered; reverential wonder; sense of mystery.

9 **Pain:** discomfort, uneasiness, disagreeable feelings not reaching the intensity of fear.
10 **Fear:** terror, dread (including frightening feelings like vertigo or claustrophobia which were sometimes mentioned).

Some of these, such as melancholy, pain and fear, are familiar in youth fiction. But there is a difference between the usual fictional descriptions, which tend to be of psychological and emotional distress, and the realities Paffard's respondents describe, which are more spiritual in nature. By that I mean that they are enlightening, enlivening and uplifting in their effects on their witnesses rather than degrading and depressing.

Under each category, Paffard quotes many brief extracts from his respondents' lengthy replies. But he also includes some of the longer accounts. Here is one example: 'Alan', aged nearly twenty, wrote about a moment of epiphany when he was sixteen and a half. An only child who lived in the country, he was not a member of any religious group but had been so until he was sixteen. He was keen on writing because 'it soothes and calms an urge to create something beautiful':

> I was on holiday, camping and canoeing in N. Wales. It was my last day there and I met a girl. We spent the day walking and talking and just being silent. Twice that day I had a strange feeling of peace, calmness and of eternity. We sat on a cliff and looked down onto the golden sands with people on them, small figures handling canoes. And as we talked I had a strange impression that time had stood still – that all the world around had ceased to move. I waited for it to pass but it persisted for the rest of the day, and I could not forget one detail of the time I had sat on the cliff top. I knew I could not forget this day – and it still only seems like yesterday. Time

seemed suspended until I had to leave; and then it was all over. I knew it could not happen again. The predominant feeling, the most lasting impression is one of calm, of security and of happiness. I remember how the sky changed – a brilliant afternoon, a summer evening and a grey, misty, wet night. I wondered if my life was to be like that; and I couldn't find an answer. I only knew that what I felt at that moment I would perhaps never feel again.

Examples of briefer extracts from long responses, which exemplify various kinds of epiphany. They are given without details about their authors' backgrounds:

A seventeen-year-old schoolgirl: When I had barely woken up one morning, I was idly wondering about heaven. I suddenly knew without any doubt at all that heaven was here. For what could only have been a fraction of a second I felt perfect joy and saw perfect light. I can't relive the feeling but only remember it because the experience was so far from ordinary feeling that I can't feel it again. It was as though my usual practical side had ceased to function for a short time. At the time it gave me a feeling of absolute certainty that if you believe in anything enough you can do it however practically impossible it may seem. I didn't think of it as a religious experience and it didn't seem to tie up with religion. As a result I have found so much in orthodox religion to be incompatible with my feelings on it that I don't belong to any religion.

An eighteen-year-old schoolboy: When I am running on a cross-country run I force my body to its utmost limits purposely. I do not do this out of any desire to win the race neither am I a very good runner. I do it because when a certain stage has been reached, the pain which racks my body becomes a gloriously wonderful thing. It is as if I am in another world. Countryside which would normally seem drab becomes exceedingly beautiful and an amazing amount of detail of the country through which I am passing sticks in my memory. Often, looking back on a run, small insignificant details stick in my mind, such as a twig which brushed my arm and the way the water runs over the stones at a certain part of a brook. Occasionally I go out of my way to meet it by running at night and this is an even more exhilarating and sometimes strangely frightening experience.

A seventeen-year-old schoolgirl: At my present age, Nature has a great effect on me. It is only recently that I have discovered that more and more I prefer to go for long walks alone or with a dog in the country. Before my exams this year, I took a book to study and went walking in the woods near my home. The book was one of Shakespeare's plays. I sat down on a log and began to read, and as I did so my mind became oblivious to what was happening around. I sat like this for so long that it became dark without my realising it and I was quite surprised when disturbed by some people walking past. It was the most enjoyable evening I have spent in recent years. It seemed that my reading blended perfectly with nature.

Thinking of all these 'marks of youth' I'm reminded of the famous letter written by John Keats to his brother George between Sunday 14 February and Monday May 3, 1819. In it he states that 'Nothing ever becomes real till it is experienced'; discusses at length his understanding of how people achieve their identity; suggests we call the world 'The Vale of Soul-making', a memorably beautiful phrase; and offers a metaphor for what he confesses he only dimly perceives:

> I will call the world a School instituted for the purpose of teaching little children to read – I will call the human heart the horn Book used in that school – and I will call the Child able to read, the Soul made from that school

and its hornbook. Do you not see how necessary a World of Pains and troubles is to school an Intelligence and make it a Soul? A Place where the heart must feel and suffer in a thousand diverse ways! ... If what I have said should not be plain enough, as I fear it may not be, I will put you in the place where I began in this series of thoughts – I mean, I began by seeing how man was formed by circumstances – and what are circumstances? – but touchstones of his heart – ? and what are touchstones? – but proovings of his heart? – and what are proovings of his heart but fortifiers or alterers of his nature? and what is his altered nature but his soul? – and what was his soul before it came into the world and had These proovings and alterations and perfectionings? – An intelligence – without Identity – and how is this Identity to be made? Through the medium of the Heart? And how is the heart to become this Medium but in a world of Circumstances?

Keats was twenty-four when he wrote this, still in the age between. One of the quintessential youths, along with Anne Frank, Raymond Radiguet, Françoise Sagan, Mary Shelley, Clarice Lispector, Françoise Mallet-Joris, and the other astonishing youthhood authors whose poems and novels and belles lettres are acknowledged as great literature, he provides proof of the range and profundity of what people of the age between are capable of perceiving, feeling, thinking, and writing. Evidence that helps us judge the attempts by older mature adult authors to compose narratives of youthful characters who are in the vale of soul-making. Not a literature about them, but a literature of their own.

All these marks of youth are to be found in the most famous presentation of all, *The Tragedy of Romeo and Juliet*. The language, not of the street, but of a richness adolescents of any sensitivity wish they could attain. The intensity of youthhood passions. The obsessive self-analysis. The sometimes violent, always disturbing fluctuation of moods. The gripping power and demanding loyalties of the peer group. The torments of infatuation, which Romeo lingers over at length when we first meet him, and its fickleness, as when he instantly forgets the woman he thought he was in love with the moment he claps eyes on Juliet: 'Did my heart love till now?' The de-identification from family. The rebellious challenge of accepted mores. The potent mix of extreme erotic desire and naïve romantic devotion that can brew up, as it does in the play, seriously dangerous life-threatening behaviour.

No fictional exploration of the natural history of youth has told it better. It's a benchmark for youth literature because everything in it is expressed through the consciousness of youth, including the adults, who are portrayed as Romeo and Juliet perceive them, not as they see themselves and we would see them, if the play were about them. We never hear their inner thoughts as we do Romeo's and Juliet's. We are never shown other sides of their characters, no scenes offer insights into their motivations, other than those which directly affect the young lovers and of which they are aware. This is the world of burgeoning youth that is boundaried from a mature perception of other people and the world they have not yet grown into.

Because of the way Shakespeare inhabits the private soliloquised thoughts of Romeo and Juliet, and their dialogue with each other and the adults, and shows everything from the point of view of the young lovers, the audience – whether youths or older – understand what Romeo and Juliet do not: the reasons for their behaviour, the wisdom or otherwise of what they and the adults do, and the ethical aim of the tale which the title indicates: the tragedy of Romeo and Juliet. By reflecting on the misjudgements of just about everyone in the play, from the rivalrous parents to the Nurse and Friar Lawrence, from the death caused by warring boy gangs to the deaths of the star-crossed lovers, we viewers of the drama, knowing more than any of the characters, can draw conclusions about life and how to live it and why, and apply them to ourselves. If we pay heed, the play helps us to extend what we are.

We know Story is evolutionary of human nature. Literature is its most potent enactment. It can be boundary-breaking. To repeat: one of my main proposals about youth fiction is that by infusion narrative devices can bring multiple points of view into play. Characters can be convincingly shown to know and understand more than the biological and experiential confines of most real-life everyday youths.

References
David Bainbridge, *Teenagers: A Natural History*, Portobello Books, 2009. Pages 137-8, 191, 195.
Ian Hamilton, *In Search of J.D. Salinger*, Heinemann, 1988
John Keats, *The Letters of John Keats, 1814-1821*, ed. Hyder Edward Rollins, Harvard U P, 1958. As reproduced from lewisiana.nl/painquotes/keats-on-soul-making.pdf.
Richard Hoggart, 'Why I Value Literature', in *Speaking to Each Other*, Chatto & Windus, 1970. Page 11.
Michael Paffard, *Inglorious Wordsworths*, Hodder & Stoughton, 1973. Pages 226, 163-4, 107, 150, 140, 185.
William Shakespeare, *Romeo and Juliet, The Complete Works*, Riverside Second Edition, Houghton Mifflin, 1997. I.v. 52
Maryanne Wolf, *Proust and the Squid*, Harper Collins, 2007
Tales of Literacy for the 21st Century, Oxford University Press, 2016
Reader, Come Home, Harper Collins, 2018

CHAPTER 7

YOUTH AND THE LIMINAL

I've always been intrigued by people and places that are between one place, one group, one state of being and another. And I have felt, from childhood, that I'm neither one thing nor another, an outsider who belongs to no group and to nowhere. Always in a state of becoming. Perhaps that's one reason why I've been drawn to that period of life which I've dubbed 'the age between' and why I've written fiction about it. Such places and people, and indeed my novels, are in a liminal condition.

The word liminal comes from the Latin *limen*, meaning 'a threshold'. The folklorist Arnold Van Gennep devised the term liminality in his 1909 book *Rites of Passage*. He meant those communal rituals which mark, celebrate and assist the passage of individuals and small communities from one stage of life to another, especially rituals to do with the initiation of youths into adulthood.

Victor Turner developed Van Gennep's concept during the 1960s. For him the *liminal personae*, the 'threshold people', are essentially ambiguous. Their sense of identity is in flux, shifting and changing. They can feel disorientated, but also aware of new possibilities, ways of seeing, thinking and behaving. It's a period of change; of conscious reconfiguration, self-assertion, kicking over the conventional and accepted traces, a reordering of self as against society.

Youths, being neither children nor adults, are liminal people. Youthhood is a period of liminality more than any other changeful stage of life.

THE LIMINAL BEING

Why is it that youth so often receives a bad press? Everything from Shakespeare's Shepherd to my friend calling them JDs (juvenile delinquents).

What is often called cute in little children is just as often called annoying in teenagers. 'Stop being so childish,' they are told. 'Why don't you grow up?' The point being that they are no longer children and are not yet mature adults. They're in the biologically uncontrollable and confusing process of growing up. Neither one nor the other.

But it's not surprising that unsympathetic adults react as they do. Explaining this liminal condition in *Teenagers: A Natural History*, David Bainbridge remarks that 'many teenagers suffer symptoms that would be considered pathological in adults.' He mentions a few: 'prolonged unhappiness, compulsive self-criticism, disordered thought processes, undirected anxiety.' At the same time, he reminds us, they also:

> ...start to tackle many mental tasks that children simply cannot attempt. They can create and manipulate abstract concepts, cope with shades of grey in arguments, generate novel arguments based on initial assumptions, approach tasks methodically and set themselves distant goals. They can also perform the powerful feat of analysing their own thought processes – generating their own ideals, criticising and improving their own thinking and analysing their own worth. And to top it all, they develop a strong social dimension to their thinking: they can analyse relationships, verbally articulate all their new thoughts to others, and 'mentalise' – create mental models of how other people think.

The brain reaches its largest size in early adolescence and then slowly gets smaller during adulthood. During adolescence the brain is discarding unwanted or unused processes, untangling what Bainbridge calls 'This unwieldy mass of writhing chaotic cortex' at the front of the brain, which has to be 'trimmed and pruned and ordered and streamlined until it has the potential to think like a Newton, a Picasso or a Presley'. The biological purpose of the ten years or more of youthhood is to allow time for the brain to completely redesign itself. This being so, it's no surprise that youthhood is a time of volatility.

Youth fictions dramatise this precarious balancing act and the price paid. But in my opinion they too often concentrate only on emotionally and physically sensational episodes, and neglect those other key aspects of youthhood which interest me the most and interest many youths: the cognitive, linguistic, and intellectual, the rich experience of fecund language and complex thought and spiritual awakening that are an important – I'd say vital – part of youthhood. Of which, to my mind, *The Diary of Anne Frank* is one of the best examples.

ANNE FRANK AND THE LIMINAL

Anne Frank wrote her diary between the ages of thirteen and fifteen. For all but the first two months she lived in hiding in the secret annexe, the upstairs rooms at the back of the Amsterdam canalside building where her father's business was housed at 263 Prinsengracht. A Jew born in Germany, she was moved at the age of four with her family to Holland. She wrote her diary not in German, her mother tongue – which she refused to use out of hatred for what was being done to her people – but in Dutch, her second language.

A Jew living in an adopted country which was occupied by an enemy who intended her people's extermination, hidden in the confined space of a few small rooms which were not supposed to exist: everything about her was betwixt and between. As an adolescent she was between childhood and adulthood. As a German Jew living in Holland she was between one country and another. As a fugitive she was in limbo, unable to go outside or do any of the things teenagers usually do. Because of her death at sixteen in the abyss of a Nazi concentration camp, she would remain always becoming, always unfinished, always between one state, one condition, one culture, one nation, one way of life, even one language and another.

Intended as a secret record of her daily life, her diary is now internationally public in every detail. It was begun in a conventional style, but during the last few weeks before her capture she started to rework it as a novel. So as a form of writing it was between one kind and another. But both as diary and novel it was left unfinished; arrested, like herself, in a state of becoming.

This is true even of her death. She was last seen when fatally ill with typhus, lying with her sister Margo on the vulnerable bottom bunk immediately inside the door of a hut in Bergen-Belsen, about two weeks before the camp was discovered by British soldiers. At that time she lived betwixt and between: in the biological condition that is adolescence; in the cold and draught of the bunk by the door of the hut where she died in the few limbo days between the German guards leaving and the arrival of the liberating troops.

Anne Frank personifies what it means to be liminal. I first read her diary in my early twenties. As a writer of youth fiction I take it as my benchmark; a best example which records in her own words what an intelligent youth in her early teens is capable of recording in vivid detail and in arresting everyday language, her thoughts, feelings, desires, conflicts of heart and mind, her joys, her spiritual epiphanies, her longings and ambitions, her anger and irritations over other people and the world, her developing sexuality and feminism, her political stance and her compassion, her shifts between childish behaviour and a maturity of wisdom that goes well beyond what some people think is possible for an adolescent, early teenage girl.

Whenever anyone questions, as they sometimes do, the

reality of the youth characters in my books, claiming they are unlike 'typical teenagers' (who and what are typical teenagers?), that they think and feel more deeply and more self-consciously than real everyday teenagers are capable of doing, I refer them to Anne Frank as proof of what is possible.

Written on July 15, 1944, when she was fifteen years and one month old, this entry is a clear statement of interior self-recognition as well as evidence of the maturity of thought that someone in the age between is capable of expressing in everyday language:

> I have one outstanding trait in my character, which must strike anyone who knows me for any length of time, and that is my knowledge of myself. I can watch myself and my actions, just like an outsider. The Anne of every day I can face entirely without prejudice, without making excuses for her, and watch what's good and what's bad about her. This 'self-consciousness' haunts me, and every time I open my mouth I know as soon as I've spoken whether 'that ought to have been different'; or 'that was right as it was'. There are so many things about myself that I condemn; I couldn't begin to name them all. I understand more and more how true Daddy's words were when he said: 'All children must look after their own upbringing.' Parents can only give good advice or put them on the right paths, but the final forming of a person's character lies in his own hands.

This is a soliloquy revealing the speaker's self to herself, and to the eavesdropping reader, which is as perceptive as any by a character in Shakespeare, even the most psychologically self-knowing as the guilt-haunted Macbeth and the philosophically sublime Hamlet included.

Anne Frank is a quintessential youth. What she records is what every reasonably aware adolescent feels at one time or another. Saying it as well as she does is exceptional. But then, isn't one of literature's functions to say better for us what we cannot say so well for ourselves? To speak for us. And to speak us into a state of consciousness that is greater, more aware, more profound, than we can manage without it. Which is why I say Anne's *Diary* is such a fine model of what is possible in the creation of youth literature.

References
I have written about Anne and translations of her diary in the essay 'Anne Frank's Pen', in *Reading Talk*, Thimble Press, 2001.

David Bainbridge, *Teenagers: A Natural History*, Portobello Books, 2009. Pages 187, 131, 87.
Anne Frank, *The Diary of Anne Frank*, trans. B.M. Mooyaart-Doubleday (1954), Pan Horizons, 1989

CHAPTER 8
RECOGNITION

It's a sensible proposition that a major theme of youth fiction is recognition. This is hardly surprising, if we accept that at the heart of youthhood is the compelling impulse to identify who and what you are, and could be, and why. I mention this in connection with Ian Hamilton's reading of *The Catcher in the Rye* in the chapter 'Holden and Cecile'.

The traditional recognition story is out of fashion among literary critics because it requires closure. The plot ends when the solution of the mystery is revealed. And these days that's thought outmoded. In postmodern dogma there can be no such thing as closure. There never can be a 'satisfactory' end. No mystery – not the smallest personal mystery nor the mystery of the universe – can ever be resolved. The best dramatic example of this is surely Beckett's *Waiting for Godot*, in which the mystery of who Godot is and why Vladimir and Estragon are waiting for him is not revealed and Godot never arrives. The resolution Vladimir and Estragon and the audience are waiting for never occurs. It seems the ethical aim is to demonstrate that irresolution is a permanent condition of human life. That we are on our own, alone. And that affectionate companionship is all that sustains us.

The fiction where we find traditional recognition alive and well is in the detective story, whether the detective is police, private eye, little old lady in a village, secret spy, or whatever. Which is perhaps why it is such a popular genre. People enjoy recognition stories because, whether literary critics and philosophers like it or not, people long for resolutions to vital questions, which they find in their preferred fictions if not in life.

For the sake of clarity, let's rehearse what we mean, in literary usage at least, by 'recognition'.

The word comes from Latin *recognitio*, and from *recognoscere*: to know again. Which means not only a change from ignorance to knowledge but also a change in which there is a recovery of something once known, the significant importance of which was not understood at the time.

Aristotle in his *Poetics* II, 4, calls it *anagnorisis* and says it's a change, producing friendship or enmity among those marked for good or ill. The word 'marked' is important because in classic recognition stories, as Terence Cave explains, 'signs, marks or tokens are a distinguishing feature of recognition plots – their signature, perhaps'. For example, Odysseus is identified by a scar from a wound received during a boar hunt.

In Greek tragedy the protagonist usually discovers the identity of another character who is connected to himself and the nature of his predicament. This leads to a resolution of the mystery in a denouement. Examples are Sophocles' *Oedipus*, Shakespeare's *Comedy of Errors*, *A Midsummer Night's Dream*, *The Winter's Tale* and *The Tempest*. Examples in the Modernist canon are Henry James's *The Ambassadors*, Joseph Conrad's *Under Western Eyes*, and James Joyce's make-use of the Greek model in *Ulysses*.

Umberto Eco's *The Name of the Rose* is a parody of the recognition story. It pretends to be a detective story because that is a 'respectable' form for a high-literary critic to play with. But as he is a high-literary critic and a formalist, we surely know he's playing a game of double-bluff. He is pretending to write an entertaining detective story that is a parody of the classic recognition story. In doing so he revises the genre and writes what can then be treated both as entertainment for the naïve reader (one that can be made into a popular Hollywood-style movie) and a piece of postmodernist high-lit. A fiction that satisfies the desire to be a populist writer (and a bestseller) while at the same time enjoying the ludic pleasure of an elite literary and linguistic academic.

The defining features of recognition stories are most clearly to be found in Shakespeare's plays. These are:

> ...severance in time and space, conflict of generations, mental alienation, accident, the telling of stories false and true, the status of dreams, riddles, prophecies and ghosts – and they exhibit them openly, often as the prime currency of the characters' dialogue ... the knowledge lost and recovered in recognition plots is characteristically (though not always overtly) connected with sexual knowledge; the rejoining of the strands of plot in the *anagnorisis* takes the form of couplings, tragic, comic or romantic. The figure of recognition is the pair or twin, a fused antithesis of which the hermaphrodite or androgyne would be the mythical equivalent. In this figure of a problematic 'identity', the other becomes disturbingly or reassuringly the same.

I'm quoting Cave, to whose invaluable *Recognitions: A Study in Poetics* I'm indebted in writing *The Toll Bridge*, and for the geography of this chapter.

In the old stories, overtly stated recognitions occur at the end. But in the modern paradigm, because the plot of a story is not necessarily arranged according to the chronology of events, the recognitions can be revealed both to the characters and to the readers at any point in the story. Most important of all in the new mode the main interest is in internal *anagnorisis* – the psychological states and the interior lives of the characters – rather than in plotful action. For me, the best modern demonstrations of this are in the youthhood parts of James Joyce's *Portrait of the Artist as a Young Man* and D.H. Lawrence's *Sons and Lovers*.

How does all this play out in youth fiction? I offer a personal reference.

I designed *The Toll Bridge* as a recognition story. In order to revise the traditional treatment so that the offence of closure could be turned to new advantage, the device I hit upon was the conjuror's trick of misdirection. The plot is arranged so that it appears to be Adam's story. He's the mysterious intruder who, in the middle of the night on Hallowe'en, breaks into the toll house where seventeen-year-old Jan is asleep on his own. Adam is soaking wet and dressed in nothing more than an old army combat cape. Who is he, where has he come from, why is he all but naked and without possessions? The answers are revealed by the end of the novel. Superficially, therefore, this seems to be Adam's story.

But it isn't. It's Jan's. He's the first-person focalising narrator until he's joined in the telling by Tess, the third character in a triangle of companionship. She takes over the telling of the story from her point of view for a while, before she and Jan continue together in their combined third-person voice. I intended this to unsettle the singular point of view, now outmoded, adding multiple and relative understandings to the narrative, which accord with the contemporary assertion that no single view of anything is sufficient. Along the way Jan and Tess experience moments of recognition, realisations about themselves, each other, their parents, and life itself.

The story narrates the liminal condition of two boys and a girl living through the age between while located in a liminal place, a remote toll house beside a bridge and a river. Jan, Tess, and Adam tell each other stories both true and false. Their recognitions are connected with couplings; tragic, comic and romantic. Sex, rivalry, friendship, immature and mature love, loyalty, duty, working for a living, de-identification from parents, and the desire for autonomy are all involved. The problematic 'identity', of themselves and of each other, is at times disturbing and reassuring. The 'sign' is a token necklace. The wound is not physical but psychological: Adam's condition known as the 'fugue' state. The ethical aim is to foreground the cost of becoming adult, the toll you pay to cross the bridge that takes you from adolescence to maturity.

By the end we know what has happened to Adam and why. But what we thought we knew about Jan is so unsettled we are left wondering about him, his personality, his sexuality, the nature of his relationship with Tess and his parents, and his aims for his future. The more we learn about him the more we need to know. There is no closure to his story.

Reviewers exemplified naïve readings, as they so often do with youth fiction. Some regarded the story as a traditional mystery about Adam and mentioned the 'twist' at the end and the surprise of it. Some asserted that the novel was spoilt by the end, because, they claimed, it wraps everything up and 'tells all'. None mentioned that it's a recognition story, and that it's Jan's story rather than Adam's.

It's worth reminding ourselves that in Greek etymology *anagnôstês* means 'reader'. So, in a modern treatment it's what the story leads the reader to recognise about him or herself that is as important as the characters' recognitions. As Paul Ricoeur puts it, 'The pleasure of recognition is therefore both constructed in the work and experienced by the reader ... This pleasure of recognition, in turn, is the fruit of the pleasure the spectator takes in the composition as necessary or probable.' This might remind us of Wolfgang Iser's concept of the 'implied reader', but incorporates, as Ricoeur says, 'a flesh and blood reader capable of pleasure.'

In other words, the modern recognition story has as much to do with the recognition it generates in the flesh-and-blood reader about him- or herself as it has to do with the recognition the fictional characters experience.

We need to keep in mind that characters in fictions are still read as having separate identities from each other, like people in the 'real' world. But these days we know they are 'splits' of the author. They are imagined aspects of one being. (Flaubert: 'Madame Bovary is me'.) We can read characters as themselves and discuss them as discrete persons, as is usual in everyday gossip and in humanist literary criticism. But we can also discuss them as aspects of one human being.

Which is to say that a narrative is a living body, an organic self, a being of whom the characters, including the author-and-reader-in-the-book, are a part. And so, the narrative is itself an *anagnorisis*. Any narrative, a novel especially, is an objectification (a made thing, an artefact) of the subjective experience of a living person, the flesh-and-blood author. And the story is the site of experience which the flesh-and-blood reader recreates in him or herself.

By creating the object-narrative both the author and the reader are enabled to contemplate his-or-her subjectivity and come to a better understanding of his-or-herself. Jerome Bruner calls this the subjunctivising nature of literature.

This brings us to another proposition, which I will discuss in the next chapter.

References
Terence Cave, *Recognitions: A Study in Poetics*, Clarenden Press, Oxford, 1988. Pages 250, 273.

Anne Frank, *The Diary of Anne Frank*, trans. B.M. Mooyaart-Doubleday (1954), Pan Horizons, 1989. Pages 115-6.

Paul Ricoeur, *Time and Narrative*, Volume One, trans. Kathleen McLaughlin & David Pellauer, University of Chicago Press (1984), 1990. Page 49.

CHAPTER 9
THE ADOLESCENT IN THE ADULT

If we think that youth fiction is meant only for youth readers we might as well say that detective stories are meant only for detectives, or romances between doctors and nurses set in hospitals, such as my mother obsessively read in her old age, are meant only for hospital doctors and nurses.

Presumably readers of detective stories gain a variety of pleasures. Perhaps the vicarious one of imagining themselves in the role of detective or criminal. Or the pleasure of solving a riddle before the solution is revealed. Or, just as likely, the pleasure of contemplating the ethical and moral questions the stories raise. Such as: Is murder ever justifiable and if so in what circumstances? How would I behave if I were faced with these dilemmas and why?

If youth fiction is not meant only for youth readers, why would mature adults read it for themselves rather than only for professional reasons, such as teachers and librarians when they choose fiction for pupils and youth libraries?

The same question might be asked of authors of youth fiction, unless their declared aim is to write for a youth readership only. Though even then, there is a question to be asked about why they choose that readership rather than writing for adults.

In fact many of them go out of their way, as I do, to declare that they do not write for youth readers only, but are writing stories which happen to be about characters in the age between but which they intend to interest adult as well as youth readers.

What can youth fiction do for adult readers that other forms of literature can't, or can't do as well? And if recognition, in the sense of *anagnorisis* described in the last chapter, is central to youth literature, what is it that adult readers recognise when reading it? A number of questions are here bundled together under the category of recognition.

Who writes youth fiction and why?

Who reads youth fiction and why?

What recognitions do writers and readers find in fictions determined by a youthhood consciousness?

As you cannot read anything until there is something to read, it makes sense to begin with the writer.

A RIFF ON WRITERS AND AUTHORS

I need to make the distinction I mentioned in the chapter 'Beginnings'.

I say 'the' writer but of course there is no generalised writer. Writers are as various in nature and motivations, in ambition and purpose, as are all human beings. Writing is not a profession. Nothing is being professed. There is no shared code of practice, no governing body, no regulation, no agreed training, no agreed ethical or moral standards. It's an occupation without norms.

I want to leave aside journalists and all those who write to achieve some other purpose than the creation of a literary artefact for its own sake. These I call writers. A writer makes a text into what he or she wants it to be in order to achieve an extra-textual aim – money, perhaps, or fame, propaganda, the communication of a message, the conveying of information.

I want to concentrate on those who work at an art form. I call them authors. They exercise an authority, which is the production of an inalienable text, created for its own sake, and which is not to be tampered with, changed, or in any way altered by those who choose to read it.

In creating a text an author has to find out what this text wants to be. Often, the author discovers this only during the writing of it, without knowing or understanding at the time why it must be like that. The aim is entirely to do with the creation of the text without regard to what might become of it, or of its author, when it's finished.

Authoring a text is a form of experience itself, not merely a means of coming to terms with experience. It's a compulsive activity, perhaps a neurotic activity. Authors often feel they have no choice about what they do or even the books they write. And, if they are like me, they get ill if they don't write something that matters to them.

At the same time authoring is an act of contemplation of that which is being made while it's being made.

Writers write to make a living. Authors write in order to make it possible to go on living.

Writers address a known audience and seek to please it. Authors address an audience of one, who we have come to recognise as 'the implied reader', the reader in the book.

Authors express all this in different ways.

Marguerite Duras, for instance, says that the task of the author is to 'convey the sound of the soul'. George Steiner says that 'In the arts, in music, in the philosophic moment, and in almost the whole of serious literature, solitude and singularity are of the essence.' And it is 'through poetics that human consciousness experiences free time.' An interviewer asked Philip Roth whether he shared the ideal of the author as a hermit secluded from life for the sake of art. Roth replied:

> Art is life too, you know. Solitude is life, pretending is life, supposition is life, contemplation is life, language is life. Is there less life in turning sentences around than in manufacturing automobiles? Is there less life in reading

To the Lighthouse than in milking a cow or throwing a hand grenade? The isolation of the literary vocation – the isolation that involves far more than sitting alone in a room for most of one's waking existence – has as much to do with life as accumulating sensations, or multinational corporations, out in the hurly-burly. It seems to me that it's largely through art that I have a chance of being taken to the heart at least of my own life.

There are key words here: 'vocation' and 'contemplation'. Authoring is both. And a statement of self-recognition: that in authoring a text Roth can be taken to the heart of his own life. Lev Tolstoy, who knew as much as anyone about the nature of authorial creation, had this to say in an article on Maupassant:

An artist is an artist for the very reason that he sees the objects, not as he wants to see them, but as they are. The bearer of talent – man – may make mistakes, but the talent, as soon as the reins are given to it, as was done by Maupassant in his stories, will reveal and lay bare the subject and will make the writer love it, if it is worthy of love, and hate it, if it is worthy of hatred.

Of course, the distinction between writers and authors is not rigid. On occasion, a writer can turn author, and vice versa. Sometimes a text begun as written surprises the writer by shifting him or her into the act of authoring. I have experienced this myself. But the distinction is useful here because I'm not dealing with the sociology of fiction, or its educational application in schools, or bibliotherapy. These may be interesting but they are making use of fiction as a tool to other ends, detached from an understanding and practice of it as the art of literature.

During a pause from drafting the above passage – with the serendipitous luck that is more exciting than anything planned – I happened to come upon remarks by a novelist for whom I have considerable admiration, J.M. Coetzee. His remarks sum up what I'm trying to propose about authors and readers, their recognitions, and the procedures of writing and reading. About reading he says:

> There is a dead reading and a living reading. Dead reading, in which the words never come alive on the page, is the experience of many children, those children [and youths] who never, as they say, learn to love reading. It is not impossible to learn by means of dead reading, in a rote kind of way; but in itself it is a barren, unappealing experience. Living reading, on the other hand, strikes me as a mysterious affair. It involves finding one's way into the voice that speaks from the page, the voice of the Other, and inhabiting that voice, so that you speak to yourself (your self) from outside yourself. The process is thus a dialogue of sorts, though an interior one. The art of the writer [author], an art that is nowhere to be studied though it can be picked up, lies in creating a shape (a phantasm capable of speech), and an entry point that will allow the reader to inhabit the phantasm.

To be emphasised: it involves the reader, and I would add the author, finding one's way into the voice that speaks from the page, the voice of the Other, and inhabiting that voice, so that you speak to yourself (your self) from outside yourself. And the author creating a shape, an entry point that will allow the reader to inhabit the phantasm.

Coetzee suggests that, as the reader reads, he/she cannot help creating an image of the author, which image is in itself a fiction, and that the author creates a fiction of the reader (who I call the reader-in-the-book). He also suggests that there is a kind of dialogue between the two as the author writes and the reader reads. In a summarising remark about the relationship of author and reader he says:

Analogous to the dialogue between the reader and the reader's fiction of the writer, in living reading, is the dialogue between the writer and the writer's fiction of the reader that belongs to the experience of writing. That is to say, someone, some phantasm of the reader, is spoken to and speaks back as the words go down on the page.

It is in the dual process of writing and reading that the recognitions emerge; the author's of him-herself, the characters in the story, and the reader of him-herself. As Coetzee says, this is a mysterious, creative interaction. It's the heart of a living engagement with literature that engenders an experience of multi-layered recognitions.

In youth literature the recognitions are those primarily realised for the first time and with the greatest passion and personal influence while living through the age between.

Authors often relive their own experience of these recognitions in their youth fiction. They re-know them and re-assess them in their stories. Terrence Cave suggests that this is a crisis of adolescence, and that it is re-enacted in the crisis of the adult author. Roth being taken to the heart of his own life, most obviously (for my purpose) in *Portnoy's Complaint*, which comes close to being a youth fiction. J.D. Salinger confessing that *Catcher* was 'sort of' autobiographical, that his 'boyhood was very much the same as Holden's'. Mark Twain revising himself as Huck. Marguerite Duras conveying what she calls 'the sound of her soul' in the version of her teenage self she plumbs in *The Lover*, if 'soul' is taken to mean 'the essence of your being'.

What occurs during the writing and the reading of the *anagnorisis* which is dramatised in the fiction is a renovation of the crisis for both author and reader, whether youth or adult.

To sum up why adults read youth fiction:
First, the best is as good as the best of 'adult' literature.

You read it for the sake of its value as a work of literature. And yet, because of the nature of its determination by an active consciousness of youth, it's different from adult literature. Therefore it increases the range of your reading, of your thinking, and of your perception.

Second, it reconnects you with your youth, helping you to re-evaluate and understand better what happened to you then, and what has happened to you since that might be a consequence of your experiences in the age between.

References
Laure Adler, Marguerite Duras: *A Life*, trans. Anne-Marie Glasheen, Victor Gollancz, 2000. Page 180.
J.M. Coetzee & Arabella Kurtz, *The Good Story: Exchanges on Truth, Fiction and Psychotherapy*, Harvill Secker, 2015. Page 179.
Philip Roth, *Reading Myself and Others*, Vintage Books, 2001. Pages 109-10.
Tolstoy quoted in Viktor Shklovsky, *Energy of Delusion: A Book on Plot*, trans. Shushan Avagyan, Dalkey Archive Press, 2007. Page 37.
George Steiner, *Grammars of Creation*, Faber & Faber, 2001. Pages 181, 59.

NARRATIVE STRATEGIES

CHAPTER 10
INFUSION

These days, most youth fiction is narrated in the first person, usually the voice of the protagonist or a young character observing the events and commenting on them. I've used it myself in *Dance on My Grave* and *This Is All*, and combined it with a third-person voice in *Breaktime*, *Now I Know*, and *The Toll Bridge*.

But it's a voice subject to awkward limitations, because it restricts the point of view to what the focalising narrator can witness, when it would often be advantageous for the reader to know more than the narrator can know. Thus, one feature constantly to be faced is the question: How can a story written in the first-person voice of its young narrator include a greater understanding of life than an immature youth can usually achieve in real life?

An author can choose to depict only the unsettled, limited state of youthhood, as Salinger does in *The Catcher in the Rye*, including the confusion of consciousness, and leave it at that; or the author can choose to give the character a more mature understanding than would be the case in reality, and so create the possibility of the character being more than reality allows, as happens in *Huckleberry Finn*. In previous chapters, I've tried to show how Mark Twain achieved this feat, persuading by his narrative skill that Huck really did understand all he seems to know about life.

I call this creative process infusion.

Infuse: from the Latin *infundere*: to pour into.

The theological doctrine of infusionism states that at the

birth of each individual a pre-existing soul is implanted in your body to remain there for the duration of your earthly life. The critical term I'm proposing secularises the theological doctrine:

Infusion: a character is endowed by the author with thoughts, perceptions and emotional fluency beyond the conscious capacity of the character's real-life equivalent. By authorial skill the author persuades the reader that this character could be so gifted.

Twain infuses Huck with an understanding of life, a wisdom acquired during Twain's mature years, transposing it by craft skill into perceptions Huck could discover by himself.

Of course, this is not restricted to youth fiction. It's achieved in all literature. We witness it, for example, in Shakespeare with Macbeth, Tolstoy with Constantine Levin, D. H. Lawrence with Paul Morel, Virginia Woolf with Mrs Dalloway, Gustav Flaubert with Madame Bovary, and George Eliot with Dorothea Brooke.

In youth fiction it's indispensable because of the still formative nature and limited knowledge of life of most young people. For me, stories of youthhood must depict the unstable, unresolved, wondering, often confusing experience of the age between, while yet stating it and clarifying it, as if the characters were doing this themselves, so that their stories 'make sense'.

This is one of the creative aspects of literature. I mean, the way it develops reality. Life follows art. We are all more in ourselves because of the arts than we would be without them. And literary art, more than any other, expresses not only our actuality but also our potentiality, by which awakening we become that which did not exist in us before.

I contend this from my own experience before and after I became a serious reader in my teens, and from my observation of the same development occurring in the lives of others, most especially during youthhood. At the same time, it's worth repeating that some people in their teens are capable of extraordinary perception and of recording it. For example, Raymond Radiguet in *The Devil in the Flesh* and Anne Frank in her *Diary*. They prove that it is possible.

I want to examine a scene in *Huckleberry Finn* in order to demonstrate in detail what I mean. It's the famous long interior monologue, a stream of consciousness, in which Huck argues with himself whether or not he should betray Jim by giving him away to the authorities. Jim is not a freed slave. He's a runaway. It was against the law to aid, harbour, or protect a runaway slave. Anyone caught doing so would be subject to the harshest punishment or would be consigned, as Huck puts it, 'to everlasting fire', not to mention the far worse treatment Jim would suffer.

At the end of his self-examination Huck decides he cannot betray his friend, no matter what the consequences. This is the ethical and moral heart of the book. It comes about four-fifths of the way through the story. It's a turning point. I'd go so far as to say it's the moment when Huck becomes an adult, while yet in the age between.

By the time we read this scene, we are attuned to Huck's voice. We accept the monologue as Huck's own words and his own thoughts, feelings, moral perceptions, insights into life and human nature. But of course, they are not. They are Mark Twain's, who presents them as Huck's. In actuality, and read out of context, do we really believe a fourteen-year-old boy of Huck's uneducated and abused background, even allowing for Miss Watson's best efforts to teach him the basics and improve him, could compose a passage of such refined and clear thought? The careful logic of the argument, the accomplished use of substantive and dependent clauses, and the sophisticated deployment of the semicolon surely suggest a written (not a spoken) passage composed by a skilled hand practiced at classical rhetoric and the construction of a theoretical argument. We've been seduced by the absorbing power of Twain's persuasive storytelling into accepting that this is Huck. As Thomas Cooley, the editor of the Norton edition, remarks in a footnote to this scene, and Victor A. Doyno evidences, Twain 'worked on the passage with great care, lengthening it by about 150 words when revising the manuscript. By pushing Huck the "wrong" way in a tug-of-war between feeling and conscience, he inverts a stock device of Christian rhetoric that goes back to at least St. Augustine's *Confessions* of the fourth century.'

What is it, then, that persuades us this is Huck's thinking? One feature most of all. The orchestration of the voice. By which I mean the use and placing of colloquial diction, sometimes phonetically spelt, supported by everyday turns of phrase in disturbed conventional grammar that personalise and colour the passage. As, for example:

'But I soon give up that notion'
'he'd feel ornery'
'a person does a low-down thing, and then he don't want to take no consequences'
'it ain't no disgrace'
'That was my fix exactly.'
'the more my conscience went to grinding me'
'when it hit me all of a sudden'
'that hadn't ever done me no harm'
'and ain't going to allow no such miserable doings to go only just so fur and no further'
'Well, I tried the best I could to kinder soften it up … saying I was being wicked, and so I warn't so much to blame'
'and if you'd a done it they'd a learnt you'

These are culled from only the first paragraph. Similarities are threaded all through the scene. Their cumulative effect builds up and maintains our conviction that this is Huck speaking.

Of course, the lexis must be appropriate to the character. If it isn't, the reader can't help thinking this character wouldn't say that. Getting the balance right between how much and how many kinds of these characterising idiosyncrasies to employ is a skilled procedure. Use too few and the impression that this is Huck's thinking is so thin, so obviously not his, that we lose conviction. Overdo them and the clarity of the argument is blurred by the plethora of demotic mimicry. Then the performance of the voice (as it does, for example, in *The Catcher in the Rye*) becomes the focus of interest and pleasure, not attention to the moral argument.

For me, this passage is a master class in the employment of the technique I call 'infusion'. It was especially helpful when I was writing *Dance on My Grave* in Hal's sixteen-year-old voice, as I shall go on to explain in my final chapter, 'Ways of Telling'. But first...

References
Victor A. Doyno, *Writing Huck Finn: Mark Twain's Creative Process*, University of Pennsylvania Press (1991), 1993

Mark Twain, *Adventures of Huckleberry Finn*, ed. Thomas Cooley, Norton Critical Edition, Third Edition, W. W. Norton, 1999. Pages 221-3.

CHAPTER 11
HOW TO DO MORE WITH THE FIRST PERSON

When I began writing youth fiction, I realised the limitations of the first person, and studied how it can be made inclusive of other characters' points of view, particularly those of adults. I wish I had come across the model I've since learned from the most: Rainer Maria Rilke's only novel, *The Notebooks of Malte Laurids Brigge*, published in 1910, and another of the canonical examples of *bildungsroman*.

Rilke employs a number of techniques to enlarge the scope of his twenty-six-year-old narrator; techniques which bring other characters' perceptions into the story and which are too rarely put to work in first-person youth fiction. This is how he does it:

[a] Brigge introduces a character into his story who then imparts information and perceptions Brigge does not (and could not) know. As, for example, when his mother tells him about Ingeborg, who Brigge has never met. This adds another narrative to the story from which she draws moral judgements about life and how to live it, judgments which Brigge is not experienced enough to make for himself. [Sections 27 and 28]

[b] The use of another character's account of an episode in order to include something the narrator either cannot have known, or which the character recounts in a more

mature version than the narrator is capable of. Brigge introduces one of these accounts with the words: 'And now I shall write down the story as Maman told it...' [Section 28]

[c] Direct address by the narrator to another character provides variety and a change of tone, and a different kind of reflective commentary:

> My dear Erik, you were perhaps my one true and only friend. The fact is, I never had one. It is a shame you set no store by friendship. I should have liked to tell you so many things ... I remember that your portrait was being painted at the time ... I cannot recall what the painter looked like ... I wonder if he saw you as I see you? ... [Section 35]

Erik is not present, but addressing him as if he were allows Brigge to write about friendship and himself in a way he couldn't otherwise.

Rilke sometimes shifts Brigge from addressing the implied reader to addressing another character directly, without any indication:

> I turned down one of the paths and walked towards a laburnum tree. And there was Abelone. Beautiful, beautiful Abelone. I hope I may never forget how it felt when you looked at me. How you wore your look, holding it on your back-tilted face as if it were not firmly attached ... I shall not tell anything about you, Abelone ... because only wrong is done in the telling. [Section 37]

He then goes on to tell Abelone about the room he's in, imagining her with him and how they would look at it together. The passage ends: 'Abelone, I am imagining you are here. Do you understand, Abelone? I think you must understand.' [page 121]

In all forms of communication what is told and how it is told are determined by the narrator's assumptions about the person who is being addressed.

When a narrator shifts from addressing an unspecified implied reader to a character in the story, everything changes: selection of details, tone (the relationship of the narrator to the addressee), emotional register, references that are assumed to be shared and references that must be explained, complexity or simplicity of lexis, of style. We witness all this in the differences between Brigge's voice when narrating to the implied reader and his monologue addressed to Abelone.

[d] Another story is embedded as someone else's memory:

> I shall write down what she [Abelone] remembered. There was a time in Abelone's early girlhood when she was possessed of a broad and idiosyncratic sensitivity. At that date, the Brahes lived in town, in Bredgade, and led an active social life... [Section 44]

The story is Abelone's memory but the voice is that of Brigge, addressed to the implied reader. Brigge tells us what he remembers Abelone telling him but in his own narrative voice, including indeterminacies which suggest that his retelling might be unreliable: 'if I understood her rightly'. Two points of view and two narratives are blended: Abelone's and Brigge's. This enriches the story and releases it from a narrow focus only on the narrator's knowledge, experience and understanding.

[e] Imaginative speculation is introduced in order to weave into the narrative thoughts and ideas suggested to the narrator by the plot but not essential to it. In this example, Brigge uses it for a meditation on death:

> I now understand very well, by the way, that a man will carry, for many a year, deep inside his wallet, the account of a dying hour ... Can we not imagine someone copying out, let us say, the manner of Felix Arvers's death? He died in a hospital, at ease and in repose, and the nun perhaps supposed he was closer to death than in fact he was. She called out some instructions or other, in a very loud voice, detailing where this or that was to be found. [Section 48]

[f] The narrator branches out from the story to riff for a while on a topic that interests him or her, as Brigge does in a long sardonic passage about his neighbours, their personalities and foibles, his encounters with them, and their effects on him. In fact, he uses them as examples of universal truths about life and human beings:

> There is a creature that is perfectly harmless if you set eyes on it; you hardly notice it and instantly forget it. Should it somehow get into your ears unseen, however, it begins to evolve, and hatches, as it were; there have been cases where it made its way into the brain and flourished there, with devastating effect, like the pneumococci in dogs that enter the nose.
> This creature is your neighbour.
> Now since I have been living like this in various places, on my own, I have had countless neighbours, above me and below, to the right or to the left, at times all four at once. I could simply write the history of my neighbours; that would be a life's work. True, it would be more a history of the symptoms they have caused in me; but that is something they share with all creatures of a similar sort – that their presence can only be demonstrated through the malfunctions they occasion in certain tissues. [Section 49]

This is also another example of a story within a story. The narrator might or might not answer questions this raises or might leave the resolution of them up to the reader. Why is this story told now? What is its relation to the main story? What purpose does it serve? What does it add to the whole? In this passage, Brigge finishes the riff by telling us the life-lessons he draws from the anecdote:

> After this experience, I resolved that in similar cases I would always go straight to the facts. I noticed how straightforward they were, and what relief they brought, compared with conjectures. As if I had not known that all our insights come after the fact; they draw a line under an account, and that is all. On the very next page a quite different account begins, with no balance carried forward.

[g] The narrator compares him- or herself with other people, the better to understand that self. In a long passage Brigge compares himself to people who live on the streets, like a newspaper seller he meets every day.

> It is not that I want to set myself apart from them if I wear better clothes that have always been mine, and insist on having a place to live. But I am not as far as they are. I don't have the courage to live as they do ... No, it is not that I want to set myself apart from them; but it would be presumptuous in me to think myself their equal. I am not. I should have neither their strength nor their capability. I take my meals, and from one to the next I lead a life altogether without mystery; while they subsist almost like eternal beings. [Section 60]

Of course, irony is at work here. The reader sees prejudices in the narrator's comparisons that the narrator doesn't see in himself. Declarations of self-awareness reveal unawareness to the observer. Standing behind the first-person narrator is the author. How aware is he or she of the narrator's unawareness? How much does the author Rilke know of his narrator Brigge that Brigge doesn't know of himself?

The Notebooks of Malte Laurids Brigge is rich in such ambiguities, and in techniques that widen the scope of the story beyond Brigge's first-person limitations. Which is perhaps why, among other reasons, Rilke's only novel continues to compel the attention and admiration of readers some hundred years after it was written.

References

Rainer Maria Rilke, *The Notebooks of Malte Laurids Brigge*, trans. & ed. Michael Hulse, Penguin Books, 2009. [Note: sections and page numbers are from an ebook edition and may be different in the printed edition.]

CHAPTER 12
THE THIRD PERSON

First-person narration has become the focalising voice in so much youth fiction because it is the easiest technique by which to create a persuasive illusion of a youth consciousness speaking for itself. But none of us, flesh or fiction, is enough on our own.

For me, one of the inestimable benefits of literature is that it can reveal the interpretive perceptions, the understandings, the consciousness of many different people within a story. As C.S. Lewis put it, '[I]n reading great literature I become a thousand men and yet remain myself'.

Of course, one way out of the singular trap is to include first-person narration by many characters, each telling the story from their own point of view and their own direct involvement in the plot. This enlarges the scope of knowing. Paul Zindel does it in *The Pigman*; the teenagers John and Lorraine take turns writing the story. I used the same technique in *Now I Know* and *The Toll Bridge*. But it can seem cumbersome when there are more than three first-person narrators, as in William Faulkner's *As I Lay Dying*.

Third-person narration allows more wide-ranging shifts of focus. And it allows the inclusion of an interpretative perception greater than any one character can provide. I'm avoiding the usual term for this apparently all-knowing narrator: omniscient. Because, as James Wood explains in *How Fiction Works*, omniscient narration is rarely as omniscient as it seems:

So-called omniscience is almost impossible. As soon as someone tells a story about a character, narrative seems to want to bend itself around that character, wants to merge with that character, to take on his or her way of thinking and speaking. A novelist's omniscience soon enough becomes a kind of secret sharing: this is called free indirect style, a term novelists have lots of different nicknames for – 'close third person', or 'going into character.'

Twain's creation of Huck Finn is an example of how by infusion the limitation can be expanded. But even then, the story cannot escape the confining bonds of one-person point of view to the exclusion of all others in the story. And I've tried to show in the previous chapter techniques which broaden the scope of the first person.

Which is all very well if the author's and our only interest is in the narrating character. But it's not enough if our interest is more ambitious, more wide-ranging, more curious than that.

THE CHOCOLATE WAR

Robert Cormier's youth novel *The Chocolate War* shows how an author can escape the confining bonds of a first-person youth narrator by using the third person while yet staying within the consciousness of youth.

When it was published in 1974 in the US (1975 in the UK) *The Chocolate War* caused a scandalised disturbance among reviewers, especially among adults who could not yet distinguish between books they regarded as suitable for children and those depicting the awkward realities of unfettered youth. Betsy Hearne's review in the American Library Association's *Booklist* was framed in a black border, as if it was an obituary. The British magazine *Junior Bookshelf*, while allowing that it was 'brilliantly written', decided that the book 'depicts a life without hope in which boys prey upon each other like prohibition gangsters, masturbate in the lavatory and drool over girlie magazines. It presents in one neat package all the most repellent aspects of the American way of life.'

Others grasped what Cormier was doing. Richard Peck in the US described it as 'Surely the most uncompromising novel ever directed to the "12 and up reader" – and very likely the most necessary'. And Peter Hunt in the UK wrote that it was 'A tour de force of realism ... a rather remarkable achievement', adding that Cormier's 'stock in trade' is ... to stand 'clichés (and our clichéd responses) on their heads and kick them, hard.'

With the benefit of hindsight Patricia J. Campbell sums up by saying 'it is no wonder that, when confronted by *The Chocolate War* with no other writings to put it in perspective, many critics over-reacted and saw only bleak hopelessness where Cormier had intended an uncompromising but therapeutic honesty. And they worried about the effect on young people.'

The Chocolate War is a novel of multiple voices. In thirty-nine numbered chapters, the shortest no more than one and a half pages, the longest thirteen pages in the British edition, the narrator employs free indirect style to convey the thoughts, feelings and perspectives on the story's events of thirteen characters so that we 'see things through the character's eyes and language but also through the author's eyes and language, too ... This is merely another definition of dramatic irony: to see through a character's eyes while being encouraged to see more than the character can see' (Wood).

The chapters, which are focalised by the primary character, Jerry's point of view, are irregularly interwoven with chapters devoted to other characters and some which include more than one character. The structure is handled with such skill that the course of events, chronologically arranged, is clear and dramatically logical. Each chapter develops the character and adds another step in the plot. The pattern never becomes monotonous, as it would if there was a regular alternation between Jerry and someone else.

It is Jerry's point of view that dominates, and we cannot help sympathising with him, even though he occupies only about a third of the narrative. But the skilful structure of the plot presents the other characters' points of view, a complex of perspectives that help create for the reader a sophisticated perception of the meaning of the story.

Though not the only one, Cormier's novel is emblematic of the development of the youth novel that was under way during the 1960s and rapidly gathered pace in the 1970s and 1980s. It is an instructive model of what can be done in youth fiction.

References

Patricia J. Campbell, *Presenting Robert Cormier*, updated edition, Twayne Publishers, 1989. Page 55. The reviewers' quotes are taken from pages 52-3.

Robert Cormier, *The Chocolate War*, Victor Gollancz, 1975

C.S. Lewis, *An Experiment in Criticism*, Cambridge University Press, 1969, Page 141.

James Wood, *How Fiction Works*, Jonathan Cape, 2008. Page 8-9.

CHAPTER 13
WAYS OF TELLING

One way of thinking about the functions of an author and a reader is to say that the author ravels up the story and the reader unravels it and puts it back together again.

This chapter explains how I ravelled up the stories of *Breaktime* and *Dance on My Grave*. This is my own reading of those novels, so I'd better begin by distinguishing between the three-persons-in-one who is writing this.

First of all, most obviously, there's the person who breathes, eats, behaves generally speaking in a manner recognisable as biologically human, lives with a woman called Nancy, and does all the workaday chores every ordinary person has to do.

Second, there's the man who writes books and finds to his surprise and gratification that he manages to make a living from what is for him an imperative occupation, whether he makes a living from it or not.

Inside these two is a third person, a reader who gains the greatest, though not the only pleasure in life from reading other people's writings.

As the third person, the reader, I'm only one reader among many. All reading is an act of interpretation. I mention this not only to reassert the unique quality of each person's reading but also for a more mundane reason: I'll be referring to the English-language editions of my books. I'm quite sure that the Italian, Swedish, Dutch, French, German, Chinese and other translations are different in significant ways, not only because of the language problems of translation and cultural differences, but because each translation is to some extent a reader's interpretation of the original.

So much by way of introduction.

I'm describing the narrative structure of my novels. The term countenances a wide variety of assumed meanings. My guide is Gérard Genette's clarification in *Narrative Discourse*, where he recognises three meanings of narrative structure and boils them down thus:

> analysis of narrative discourse as I understand it constantly implies a study of relationships: on the one hand the relationship between a discourse and the events that it recounts ... on the other hand the relationship between the same discourse and the act that produces it, actually (Homer) or fictively (Ulysses) ... Analysis of narrative discourse will thus be for me, essentially, a study of the relationships between narrative and story, between narrative and narrating, and (to the extent that they are inscribed in the narrative discourse) between story and narrating.

Following Genette, I'll discuss the relationship between myself as storyteller (craftsman), my fictive protagonists (Ditto in *Breaktime*, Hal in *Dance on My Grave*), the events that compose their stories, and the ways of telling that produce the narrative. Various critical insights inform what follows. Here are the words that, for me, provide their best expression. The first is from Hans-Georg Gadamer in *Truth and Method*: 'Not occasionally only, but always, the meaning of a text goes beyond its author.' The next three are from Roland Barthes' essays in *Image-Music-Text*:

'the work can be held in the hand, the text is held in language.'

'We know now that a text is not a line of words releasing a single 'theological' meaning (the 'message' of the Author-

God) but a multi-dimensional space in which a variety of writings, none of them original, blend and clash. The text is a tissue of quotations drawn from the innumerable centres of culture.'

'to read (to listen to) a narrative is not merely to move from one word to the next, it is also to move from one level to the next.'

A final quotation from Barthes serves as a link to what I want to explain: '[T]he metaphor of the Text is that of the network.'

The network that composes the structure of *Breaktime* can be drawn as a diagram read either two-dimensionally, like a theme-catching fishnet, or three-dimensionally, like a geological section through a thematic landscape (Fig 1).

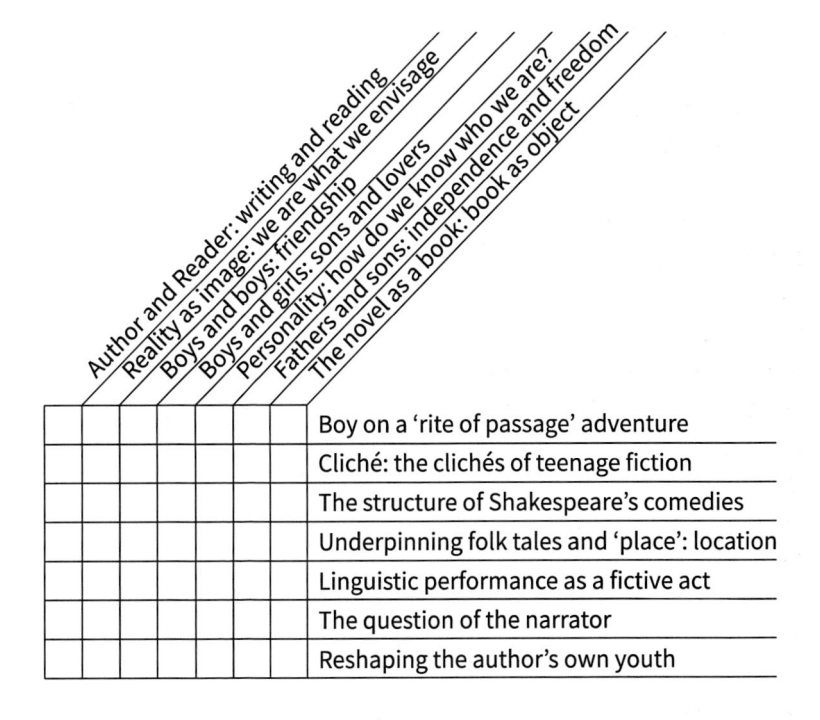

Author and Reader: writing and reading	Reality as image: we are what we envisage	Boys and boys: friendship	Boys and girls: sons and lovers	Personality: how do we know who we are?	Fathers and sons: independence and freedom	The novel as a book: book as object

							Boy on a 'rite of passage' adventure
							Cliché: the clichés of teenage fiction
							The structure of Shakespeare's comedies
							Underpinning folk tales and 'place': location
							Linguistic performance as a fictive act
							The question of the narrator
							Reshaping the author's own youth

Fig 1: Breaktime: *The network of the narrative*

Perhaps this makes the book seem foggy, far more difficult for readers than I hope it is. I think of it this way: A walker across a countryside should be able simply to enjoy the immediately visible sights without bothering about how they got to be like that. In crafting a story, I aim to provide the surface with an entertaining landscape and a path pleasant enough to satisfy uninquisitive readers. But all paths, all landscapes, acquire their features and contours from a geology that lies hidden beneath the ground. Some walkers enjoy investigating these foundations, as do some readers in their enjoyment of novels. I'm writing this for readers who like to know what is going on underground.

Breaktime's story turns on the axis of two intersecting 'surfaces'. One is the plot about a boy on a journey, a rite-of-passage adventure that takes Ditto from emotional confusion to a moment of recognition, when he sits waiting, ready for the next surge in his life.

The other, intersecting seam is the reader's adventure over the surface of the page, which presents the story as a graphematic, as well as a linguistic, experience – the typography itself, drawings, handwriting, footnotes, 'concrete' prose, and the like – in which the novel as a book, and the book as a made object decorated with marks, becomes the focus of attention, of enjoyment I hope, and is itself one of the ways of telling the story. These elements set up the warp and weft of the network. They also establish the relationship between the protagonist and the reader, who, adventuring together, each the hero of the story, encounter one another in the printed marks on the page.

I'm aware I'm mixing my metaphors. I don't, however, think of them as an inappropriate soup but as interdependent, all part of a kaleidoscope of images, none of which is sufficiently suggestive of how a novel behaves to satisfy me on its own. Besides, as a writer and a reader I do actually think of a novel as a pattern of three-dimensional shapes, also as music, and as a journey through space (landscape) and through multiplicities of time. And I am here giving as nearly as I can a truthful account of my reading of myself, even at risk of inelegant collisions in the kaleidoscope of metaphor.

If we now move down a level, we find a layer of soft clay: the clichés of youth fiction. Boy meets girl; son rebels against parents; adolescents engage in rivalries and dares and the thrills of first, surreptitious sex. We find an owl hooting, cliché symbol of death and wisdom; a cuckoo calls, cliché herald of amorality; Helen, that cliché temptress, appears before Ditto dressed quite explicitly as a 'desirable cliché' when they meet for the seduction in that cliché of romantic settings, a beautiful hillside.

Cliché fascinates me. If, as is said so often it is itself a cliché, there are no new stories, then, in a crude sense, there are only clichés from which to begin. And, as with all clichés, there's some truth in this one. Roland Barthes refines the idea by writing, 'The text is a tissue of quotations drawn from the innumerable centres of culture'. Straw and clay are clichés of earth. We make bricks of them for building new places. The new is made out of the old, and the raw material is often worn out, used up as far as its original purpose goes. In cliché, the content remains true but the way of saying it is exhausted. No new truths, just fresh – or refreshed – ways of expression.

Refreshment, reinvigoration, making the old new is achieved by a re-examination, a reworking, of the form. Literary theorists call this 'deformation'. Viktor Shklovsky put it like this: 'a work of art is perceived against a background of and by association with other works of art. The form of a work of art is determined by its relationship with other pre-existing forms ... *The new form makes its appearance not in order to express a new content, but rather, to replace an old form that has already outlived its artistic usefulness.*' [Italics in original.]

The most popular clichés are interesting because their popularity attests to their general appeal. And form preoccupies me because in form I discover energy. For me, form, the way of telling, is a composition of voice (the personality of language) and craft (the techniques by which language is given narrative expression). And I try to make my youth novels works of deformation.

It is all very well being interested in cliché and listing off those located in *Breaktime*, but every story requires a plot, a framework of events that give it shape and direction. After much fussing about at the note-making stage, when I tried to find a plot by my own unaided invention, and failing, I at last stumbled across this passage in *The 'Revels' History of Drama in English*, in which Alvin Kernan writes:

> The characteristic Shakespearean comic plot extends this perpetual hesitation between dream and thought into action. As the play progresses, the characters move, in response to their own psychic urgencies and the great powers that flow through their worlds, from familiar, well-lighted places and states of mind, into strange, unfamiliar dim places and experiences, only to return after a period of confusion, surprise and revelation to their place of origin. The movement is, to use Shakespeare's most persistent symbols, from city to wood and back to city again ... from everyday to holiday and back to everyday, from the restraints of society and order to release and freedom and then, renewed, back to work and sobriety ... from an old society which has become repressive, tyrannous and life-destroying to a revolutionary explosion, usually undertaken by youth in the name of freedom and vitality, leading to a second period of disorder and excess. This phase gives way in turn to the third period of the formation of a new society, which, while including all within its feasts and celebrations, is centred on youth and the new generation.

This gave me precisely what I was looking for, not only for *Breaktime* but for the plots of all my youth novels. Young people in rebellion against waning adult authority go off to a place inspiring of uninhibited, even licentious behaviour, where they discover themselves more profoundly than before, after which they return to the regulation and order of adulthood changed and closer to achieving their personal independence.

Discovering this controlling design led me to ask questions that were drillheads cutting into the next layer, a level deeper in the story's geology. Where would the story happen? Which town would be Shakespeare's 'city', which place his 'enchanted forest'?

I looked at the area round my present home in Gloucestershire, but wasn't happy with it as the novel's setting. I tried other familiar locations, but none was right. Finally, I thought about the part of the North East of England where I grew up, the town of Darlington, and the hills and dales a few miles away around Richmond in Yorkshire.

Given the nature of *Breaktime* you might wonder why I didn't think of this to start with. For two reasons. The first was practical. I don't much like travel, Darlington is two hundred and forty miles from my home, and I didn't want the trouble of driving there every now and then to check the facts of the location. The second reason was psychological. I feared that setting the story in the places where I spent my youth might bring my own life and the fictional lives of my characters dangerously close together. I wanted to avoid the snare always waiting for novelists, the temptation to evade problems of invention by disguising autobiography as fiction. In the event, the use of my youthful stamping ground repaid the risk by giving me an unexpected and invaluable experience that has ever since been useful to me, as I'll relate in a moment.

What finally persuaded me to settle for Darlington and Richmond was the narrative potency I discovered they possessed when I imagined Ditto's story taking place there.

To begin with, Darlington is flat, rather dull, architecturally undistinguished, and has a history associated with locomotives (the George Stephenson works were there) and the now dying glories, if glories they ever were, of the industrial revolution. What better correlative for the fading powers of adult authority and the cultural mores against which my young protagonist was to rebel?

On the other hand, the ancient little market town of Richmond, and the Pennine valley of the river Swale at the foot of which Richmond stands guard, is scenically dramatic, outstandingly beautiful, possessively enchanted, the very type of Shakespeare's Forest of Arden. Swaledale literally sparkles with energy, for the valley is dominated by the fast-flowing, boulder-strewn, lightflecking river beside which hills stride and tumble, rise and fall again and again, like topographic athletes with big muscles. Hills and river, the male and female of geography, lying together, have conceived a landscape of vigour and beauty. What more magic place, what more likely setting to release and re-form pent-up adolescent emotions?

I knew it would because it did that for me in my youth. The invaluable authorial experience this setting gave me, which I mentioned a moment ago, was discovering how to find in myself and in my own life what I call 'reference points for truth' by which to test the veracity of a character's experience during the writing of a novel. In other words, it taught me how to use myself to write truth in fiction while also keeping my distance. I don't say I can always do it, only that taking the risk showed me what fictional truth really means.

Dig deeper to the next level, and we find that Richmond offers not only a topography that supports the story but a typology too. Five local legends – five popular folk tales – are alive in the area. I was astonished by the closeness of match between their symbolic significance and the needs of my story. Absorbing these tales into the underground of the novel gave the story a richness and a focus that until then it had lacked.

These are the tales:

Robin Hood, who, as every British schoolchild believes, robbed the rich and gave to the poor, but was in fact a political dissident imprisoned – that is, made socially and politically impotent – in Richmond Castle for a time. The old spelling of Hood is Hode, the surname I gave to Robby in *Breaktime*. His impotent rebellion against his father is expressed openly in disagreements about politics and covertly through disapproved-of sexual behaviour with his friend Jack.

In the second story, a man called Potter Thompson finds his way underneath Richmond Castle where King Arthur's knights are said to lie asleep under a huge bell. If the bell is rung, the knights will wake and come to England's aid in time of need. Potter Thompson almost rings the bell but fails in courage. An old ballad gives his son's name as Jack.

Jack Thompson is the name I gave to Robby Hode's dropout friend, big of body but slight of spirit, who ducks out of the brawl at the political meeting where Robby tries to rouse the members of the socialist party from their unprotesting acceptance of the sell-out of their ideals represented by their main speaker, the man we later learn is Robby's father.

A third legend tells how a little drummer boy was ordered into an ancient tunnel that was rumoured to link Richmond Castle with Easby Abbey, two or three miles down river, thus connecting the now ruined political stronghold to the now ruined religious centre of the region. In order to plot the course of the tunnel the boy was told to walk through it, beating his drum loudly, while the adults listened on the ground above and followed his track. The boy did as he was told, and was heard drumming for a while, but then the noise ceased and he was never heard or seen again.

Ditto meets Robby and Jack in Richmond Castle, attends in drunken state the political meeting held in a bleak market hall – which in fact stands hard by and virtually under the castle – is knocked out during the brawl, and wakes, being sick into the Swale near Easby Abbey, after which he takes part in burgling the Hodes' house.

The paralleling of the Drummer Boy's story and these incidents is all the more obvious if connections are made between, for example, the various meanings of the verb 'to drum', which include 'to sound a summoning call', 'to obtain agreement or help', 'to inform or warn off', 'to sound out or discover the truth about'.

These three tales help locate the relationships between the characters, the events, and the themes I intend.

The fourth story is given a more explicit entrance into the novel and is about the lass of Richmond hill, subject of one of the best known folk songs in English:

On Richmond hill there lives a lass
More bright than Mayday morn

Here is cliché indeed, and in its most delightfully virulent form, the pop song! This lass, as in so many pop songs, is an idealisation of a masculine fantasy. A variant story tells us that her real-life model was a high-class whore with rotten teeth and bad breath. But was she? There's no indisputable evidence, and the variant story might perhaps be the work of a satirical misogynist or, for that matter, of some joyless female Encratite out to score a point. At any rate, she brings with her an ironic ambiguity that pleases me and benefits Ditto's story.

How, though, to absorb it? Who, I asked myself, is the classic cliché of the same type? The answer was obvious: Helen of Troy, she whose face launched a thousand ships, a reputation itself the punning butt of schoolboy jokes. So Ditto's enticing lass (and possible male fantasy), who first takes possession of him and then abandons him, became Helen, sender of snapshots and siren-song letters. (These days they'd be selfies with spiel on some social media app.)

And on which hill should they sport, there being so many? This was easily decided by another local story, the fifth. It's well documented, more news item than legend, and openly recounted in the novel without disguise from the original sources (thus helping to create Barthes' 'multi-dimensional space in which a variety of writings, none of them original, blend and clash'). The hill is the one where Robert Willance's runaway mount, galloping recklessly through fog, plunged over a sheer scarp above the Swale, and died where she fell, leaving her rider so helpless with a broken leg that the only way he could save himself was by splitting open the horse's belly and laying his wounded leg inside to keep it warm till rescue came. Afterward, he erected a monument to his horse in gratitude. No need, I think, to point out the relationship between this story and Ditto's as he and Helen ride each other beside the monument to Willance's leap on the swelling hills above the Swale, upriver from Richmond.

These stories interweave, of course; they aren't separate threads. And therefore they influence and change each other as well as Ditto's narrative. To take just one example: at the political meeting where the boys sit together, a drunken Ditto, having already 'drummed' Hode and Thompson, first thinks that he is in a dungeon, then at a prayer meeting. When he asks in his inebriated confusion whether everyone is asleep, Robby tells him that they are 'wakers asleep' who are dreaming. In this brief exchange the three subventing folk tales work together, creating a subtext that draws another pattern of the book's meanings. Immediately afterwards comes Ditto's most uninhibitedly anarchic moment described in comic-strip-like devices that also bring the graphematic features to their climax. And all this happens at the very centre of the physical book.

If the metaphor of the text is changed from a network to a wheel, this passage may be seen as the hub, with all this implies about the book's construction and the way it asks to be read. The shape is not linear, not a trajectory, like a ball being thrown from one person to another, but orbicular, like being at the centre of the wheel while it is spinning along the ground.

The last three layers take us below the structural formalities, deep into the bedrock on which the novel is constructed, where we discover the controlling themes. These extend beyond the confines of *Breaktime*, and because they are not structural but are wholly thematic in function they lie, strictly speaking, outside this discussion. However, so important are they in my own reading of the book that for satisfaction's sake I'll say something about them.

Quite obviously, the story plays with the relationship between so-called fiction, so-called fact, and language. Is Ditto telling the factual truth or has he invented the story? Can Morgan or we, the readers, know someone else's experience except through the language in which it's communicated? What are we dealing with, what are we experiencing, when we engage in the reading of a narrative? What does fictive language do?

Breaktime makes no attempt to engage in discussion of these questions. Rather, it makes a story out of them. And quite literally that story is only – is nothing but – language. It's a story about language and about kinds of language, and has no reality, for me, except as language.

Even Ditto's name signals that this is so. 'Ditto' means a repetition symbolised by two small marks ("). He is, therefore, simply a drawing, marks on a page, just as his story is nothing but writing. In a literal sense, all writing is drawing, having no reality except as the marks themselves. Thus Ditto is a tautology, a self-sustaining being who exists by indicating his own repetition. But a repetition of whom? Of no one, of course, except the being created by the language that composes his story and therefore Ditto himself.

When thought of this way, a ditto mark could be said to

be the most abstract of signs. It functions as a signifier to a signified that is another language, the language of Story itself. Which means that Ditto himself is a literary joke, just as his entire story is a comedy. And yet a reviewer in *The Times* could only find in Ditto's name 'Chambers/Ditto (get the joke?)'. That reading shows once again how readers make what they like of any writing and crudify fiction into a poor disguise for the author's own first-person life, no matter how hard the author works to make the story's independent being clear. Nor, by the way, can the *Times* reviewer have been familiar with Lewis Carroll, not to have remembered this scene from *Through the Looking-Glass, and What Alice Found There*:

'I'm afraid he'll catch cold with lying on the damp grass,' said Alice, who was a very thoughtful little girl.
'He's dreaming now,' said Tweedledee: 'and what do you think he's dreaming about?'
Alice said, 'Nobody can guess that.'
'Why, about you!' Tweedledee exclaimed, clapping his hands triumphantly. 'And if he left off dreaming about you, where do you suppose you'd be?'
'Where I am now, of course,' said Alice.
'Not you!' Tweedledee retorted contemptuously. 'You'd be nowhere. Why, you're only a sort of thing in his dream!'
'If that there King was to wake,' added Tweedledum, 'you'd go out – bang! – just like a candle!'
'I shouldn't!' Alice exclaimed indignantly. 'Besides, if I'm only a sort of thing in his dream, what are you, I should like to know?'
'Ditto,' said Tweedledum.
'Ditto, ditto!' said Tweedledee.

Language must be uttered before it can be heard. Naturally, therefore, a whole stratum of the narrative's geology, the next level down, is composed of hard-rock questions: Who is telling this story? Whose voice do we hear? Who is the narrator?

In *Breaktime* the answer is simple. It's Ditto's story, and it's his voice we hear. He's the narrator. But there's a mix of first-person and third-person voices. This was not arbitrary. To speak as the author (which a reader cannot know), the choice for each passage was considered from a number of points of view, mostly to do with the problem of the narrator rather than the technical reason that the first-person creates an effect of immediacy and closeness to the protagonist, while the third-person creates a sense of distance, of being an observer rather than a participant.

The juxtaposing of the two voices is meant to help compose a polyphony, and a duality of personality, so that the reader stands now within, and now without, the story, and 'hears' the linguistic shifts more keenly than would be the case without the use of this device. However, I must add this was not thought out before I started writing the story. It came about because Ditto wanted it that way. As I've explained in other chapters, when writing I'm 'inhabited' by the youthhood narrator. Only after I've drafted the story do I think about it in these technical terms. When I've worked out what is going on and why, I revise the text to clarify it, removing anything that clutters the narrative as inevitably occurs in a first draft.

Breaktime and others of my novels have sometimes been criticised for being, as it's usually put, 'too self-conscious'. Agreed, there's a kind of self-consciousness that is a weakness, when the writing hasn't been sufficiently absorbed by the author. But there's a kind of self-consciousness of youths like Ditto when they try to write. They imitate their favourite authors and are sometimes pompous; they can over-decorate and look for unusual words and modes of expression. They also mix conventions. This kind of self-consciousness is so typical of a boy like Ditto that no writing which is supposed to be his can avoid it. Finding this style, finding his voice, was important to me.

Another kind of self-consciousness has to do with writing that leads the reader to witness the writing itself, to be aware of it and to attend to it for its own sake. Devices like mixing first- and third-person, and some of the graphematic features in *Breaktime* are meant in part to achieve this.

Move down another layer and we reach the most difficult topic of all for me to say anything about, not least because I'm still unclear about it myself. At this level is confronted the relationship that inevitably exists between the three elements: the fictive act as a linguistic performance; the person of the narrator; and the author him- or herself. Again, we might pose the problem in questions. What has the author given the story? What has the story given the author? Where am I in this story and what am I doing in it?

Judging from the inordinate interest there is in the biographies of writers, which often exceeds interest in their books, I suspect a lot of people find this the subject that engages their curiosity the most. For now, I'll only say this: I sometimes think that what I was doing in *Breaktime* was shaping – or rather re-shaping – my own youth, re-examining it in the light of the years since then. And this is true of all the youth fiction I've written.

Now we can shift from the vertical to the horizontal axis of the diagram. We can take the walk I mentioned earlier through the landscape of the story, following Ditto, and look for the tributary narratives that, flowing together, make up the whole novel.

Very quickly, on the third page, we encounter the feature I've already talked about as the other main surface of the story: the graphematic elements that engage the reader's attention on the novel as a book, and on the book as a physical object covered with decorative, meaning-communicating marks. We find Morgan's typewriter-written document. (Bear in mind that the story is set in the late 1970s, before computers were commonplace.) Soon after we read Ditto's first interior monologue comes Helen's handwritten letter, and the italic/roman dialogue between Ditto and his mother, and so on.

Having set out on the adventure with print, we come next to the narrative that explores the story about fathers and sons and the struggle between them caused by the natural desire of the teenage son for his independence in the face of the father's sense of parental duty and love, which Ditto now finds overbearing and restrictive. De-identification has come into play.

Ditto goes to his room and the third narrative begins, the one dealing with the subject of personality. What are we? How do we know what we are? How do we make ourselves into what we wish to be? How do we perceive – how do we know – our lives? We view Ditto's room, we see him as he sees himself, through the objects with which he has surrounded himself during childhood, and which now irritate him because they reveal a person he no longer feels he is or wants to be. This narrative is about states of being. What is it like to be Ditto? What is his state of being as he experiences each event in his life?

I've tried to explain that *Breaktime* isn't so much about event or character as it is about states of being: the state of being adolescent, the state of being a son and a would-be lover, the state of being drunk, and of being an amateur burglar, of being a seducer and of being seduced, and so on. Just as Shakespeare's comic plot controls the overall narrative pattern, so the examination of each episode as a state of being controls the narrator's focus of attention. Which determines what he chooses to tell and how he tells about it.

Thus, for example, during the political meeting, the scene is produced linguistically and graphematically to convey what it is like to be Ditto mildly drunk at such a gathering, rather than to describe what happened and why, along with some narrative comment to illustrate the meaning, which would be the more familiar (readerly) convention. In my (writerly) telling, the reader must play the game of putting the pieces together, making the meaning that the telling signals but doesn't assert.

Later, during the seduction on the hillside, there are three narratives in one. The scene is printed in two columns. In one column the two narrative voices, the first- and third-person, talk simultaneously. The third-person – the voice that makes the reader stand back and think – describes the action and is set in roman type. The first-person, Ditto's own involving voice, is printed in italic and tells us what Ditto is thinking during the event. The facing, parallel column is an extract from Dr Spock's *A Young Person's Guide to Life and Love*, in which Spock says there isn't much point in trying to describe lovemaking because it is experienced as emotion and relationship rather than as action. Having said this, he goes on to describe sexual action in considerable detail. Placed alongside Ditto's narrative the two interact, turning one another into comedy.

In order to understand the scene you have to read it three times. Each time – or so I hope – it gets funnier, the action less erotic, and your attention is more and more fixed on Ditto's state of being.

But these examples have taken me away from the search for the narrative's tributaries. Immediately after observing Ditto in his room and beginning the exploration of his personality, we meet Helen through the medium of her handwritten letter and Ditto's first-person monologue as he leers at her provocative photograph. Though first hinted at in Morgan's opening line, 'I tell you no lie, Maureen Pinfold is a dream', this is the first substantial statement of the story about boys and girls and would-be lovers that equals in importance the story about fathers and sons. Blended together they can be relabelled 'sons and lovers', an intended echo of D.H. Lawrence's novel, a formative book in my own life.

Having contemplated images of Helen, with disturbing results, Ditto lays alongside hers an image of Morgan – the 'Charges against literature' – and then surveys them in relation to images of himself, the objects in his room. He thus draws the main stories together, adding at the same time the one already assumed in the first page and soon to surface again the next day, when Ditto relates to Morgan the drama of his row with his father and reconsiders what Morgan, 'his friend stretched at his side', means to him. This is the story of friendship, boy with boy, which *Dance on My Grave* takes up and develops. (I started work preparing *Dance* long before beginning *Breaktime*.) It is of course a variation on the *Sons and Lovers* theme.

We're now taken into the story of the book as a construct of images, of fiction as metaphor. Ditto's 'Document' – his reply to Morgan's 'Charges' – sets up questions about reality as image. While above and around, extra-textually so to speak, questions are being posed between author and reader: What is fiction and what is fact? How much of what we read about Ditto is fiction (that is, lies), and how much of it is 'true'? How true is this 'fiction' in a sense that speaks beyond words like 'fact' and 'fiction'? Thus, the vista at the end of our journey through the novel lays out for contemplation the relationship between author and reader, writing and reading. How do we view each other? What have we done with this book, and what has it done for us?

This completes the network of the text, at least when we read according to this metaphor. It makes a grid of squares, like a virgin crossword, inviting readers to play some kind of game on it. We might, for example, play a game of 'Connections'. Three along, four down: What is the connection between the boys and the underpinning folk tales, and how does this connection illuminate each? Five along and five down: What is the connection between the personality of Ditto and the linguistic performance of the book? Two along, two down: What is the connection between cliché and our image of reality? This is beginning to sound too much like an examination in literary criticism! What I'm trying to show are the different ways of entering into, and considering, the novel's potential meanings. And to emphasise that it isn't simply a linear structure but is, let's say, a hologram rather than a snapshot, a three-dimensional mobile, not a two-dimensional still.

So much for the hidden structure of the book. The visible architecture arranges the story into chronologically ordered episodes, each with its own, always signposting title. These are further grouped into four parts. I think of these as the four acts of a drama. They too are signposted by titles that suggest keynotes. The first, 'Challenge', indicates the fictional challenges issued between Ditto and Morgan, Ditto and his father, Helen and Ditto. But it also indicates the challenge issued between author and reader, and between Ditto and the reader, as an act of writing and reading. Part Two, 'Journey Out', speaks of more than Ditto's journey outwards from home, outwards from his inhibited self. It speaks also of the reader setting out on the reading journey.

The four-part pattern is further organised into eight dramatic climaxes. But the climaxes are not regularly distributed, which would have been monotonously symmetrical. The rhythm is actually: two, three, one, two. This pattern places the eventful dramatic weight in the first half of the book, and on the fourth climax. That is, on the second climax in the second part: the political brawl. This is the peak of the novel's rebellious drama and is placed right at the physical centre of the book.

After this, before and during the burgling of Hode's house, which doesn't carry the same action-full punch as the political brawl, Ditto 'comes to his senses'. The rest of the book is occupied with his 'happy revolution' in which he 'comes together' again, renewed, his boyness and girlness unified in the climax with Helen, his female surrogate.

This isn't the usual disposition of dramatic forces in a novel. For one thing, it places a great deal of trust on the interest readers find in the happy coming together of a character, as against their interest in confusion, disruption, and eventful action. For another, it disregards the conventional storyteller's wisdom that the dramatically strongest scene should be kept till near the end, and be followed by a rapid resolution before the reader gets bored. My arrangement was not, however, worked out as a demonstration of some theory of composition. The story dictated its own shape. My job as author was to clarify the shape by removing clutter. Only after I'd completed a draft did I realise how the structure was built.

A final word about the network as I've illustrated it. There are those who warn against it as inadequate, others who say it is overblown, and some who say it conditions readers into one, rigid view of how the book 'works'. Genette has the answer: 'The "grid" which is so disparaged is not an instrument of incarceration, of bringing to heel, or of pruning that in fact castrates: it is a procedure of discovery, and a way of describing.' If we cannot trust youth readers to speak for themselves, then there is no hope they will read for themselves either. The incomplete 'discovery' suggested here is simply my own way of trying to sort out the novel I've written.

INSIDE-OUTSIDE
I could draw a network for *Dance on My Grave* too, but we've had enough of that. Instead, let me explain how I read *Dance* and *Breaktime* as companion novels later joined, like a family, by the other four novels in what I call 'The Dance Sequence'. They share the same concerns but approach them differently.

In *Breaktime* all the workings are on show, like the innards of the Pompidou building in Paris. It is heterosexual, masculine, plain-speaking, revelatory. In *Dance* all the workings are hidden, as they are hidden in the walls of, say, a Georgian building, or under the floorboards. It is homosexual, feminine, ambiguous, aware that nothing ever means only one thing. The reader of *Breaktime* is in the position of someone standing outside, looking into the story; the reader of *Dance* looks from the inside out.

Both novels are eclectic in nature; they are collages of different ways of telling: letters, extracts from other fiction, graffiti, newspaper clippings, playscript, concrete verse and prose, cartoons, notebook entries, schoolboy essays, interior monologue, footnotes, impressionist and expressionist modes, lists, parodies – of, for example, B.S. Johnson, Kurt Vonnegut, Laurel and Hardy – and so on, as well as usual modes of first- and third-person storytelling. Each is placed against the other in order to produce a particular effect and each is chosen because it is the only solution that seemed to satisfy the narrative problem. But in *Breaktime* the ways of telling are offered openly, while in Dance they are mostly absorbed into the first-person voice of the protagonist, whose writing tends to be as secretive as it is revelatory. Scattered through the book are hidden messages, clues to unstated or coded information, word-game puzzles that are usually serious in intent.

An obvious example is the difference between the two books in treatment of sexual activity. In *Breaktime* Ditto's experiences are explicit; indeed, one of the key scenes, the seduction on the hillside, deals with the question of how to 'tell' about sex so that you communicate its wholeness without being prurient. In *Dance* Hal's experiences with Barry are referred to, you know they're happening, but they are never described. Yet anyone who follows the clues can piece together precisely what is going on. *Dance on My Grave*, both in form and content, plays with:

Ambiguity: of language, of personality, of motive;

Ambivalence: comic and serious, male and female, strong and weak, open and hidden;

Symbolic images: presented as naturalistic objects and events: the sea, for example, and mirrors, motorbikes, helmets, clothes of one kind and another and what dressing in them means, pictures, gifts. Of the symbolic events one of the most extended and detailed is the long scene with the bikers that begins with Bit 29 and ends with Bit 39 of Part Two. (The raw material for this, by the way, was taken from a maturational dream described and analysed by Carl Jung in *Man and His Symbols*);

Ways of telling our experiences: This last is one of the controlling and organizing features in the book's structure. It is, of course, a novel about obsession. Obsession with an image of ideal friendship; obsession with the unsettled meaning of words, and with the unsettling meaning of death; obsession with the ways images we fix upon about ourselves compose us – 'make us' – into the people we think we are. And above all, obsession with the telling of an experience, that imperative, universally felt desire to put into words what has happened to us in order to try and make sense of it.

This 'telling' is in itself a story-within-the-story. My personal conviction is that we are not changed by our experiences, as common wisdom has it. What changes are the stories we tell about our experiences. Until we have re-formed our lives into story-structured words we cannot contemplate and find the meaning of our lived experiences. Till then they remain in the realm of beastly knowledge. Only by turning the raw material of life into story – by putting it into a pattern of words we call literature, whether oral or written – can beastly knowledge be creatively transformed and given meaning. It is storying that changes us, not events. This conviction lies at the heart of *Dance on My Grave* as Hal writes himself into an understanding of his experience with Barry

Gorman. And it lies at the heart of all the fiction I've written and all the private diaries I've kept since I was a teenager.

Hal struggles with the questions: How do I tell about what happened so that it makes sense? How do I tell it so that the telling is true about what happened then, but is also true about what is happening now? How is the past turned into the present? How is memory made into meaning? The entire book is a reconsideration through memory; it is about memory and the shifting effects of memory. This being so, each scene must be told as a memory of then rediscovered as a reality now.

How to do it? Various narrative solutions are used. Here is an explanation of just one, which provides also an example of what I meant about the author using the writer's craft in the service of his authorial impulse. Television uses this device constantly, especially in sports programmes – that is, during its most action-packed, so-called 'live' shows. The device is Action Replay.

Even as a game of football is in progress, the viewer is shown the action replay of a goal that was scored a few seconds before. The replay will be shown in slow-motion so that we can see whether the goal was offside, or a player fouled, even while the referee is still arguing the point with the players on the field. And while the slow-motion replay is being shown, the unseen commentators remark on the way the goal was scored. That is, they recuperate the meaning and significance of the event as they see it. They act as a kind of narrator.

Of course, if the producer wants to, she or he can also use split-screen. Part of the picture will show the action replay, the other part will show the game as it continues. If this is done, we are watching the real-time present of the game – the story as it happens – and the historic present of the goal being scored – the game's immediate past recalled – both at the same time. And when we view these two time-scales together, and simultaneously hear the commentators' discussion of the events, our feelings about the game change, and our view of the real-present as it continues also changes. We have a different opinion of the game, and different opinions about it from the people who are actually there and cannot watch as we watch.

I find this fascinating and wanted to use it as a narrative device in order to try and achieve the same results in the reader that I believe occur in television viewing of this kind; with the added quality that a novel is a contemplative medium. It allows you more time to think than television does, because television is a transient and superficial medium.

Early in *Dance* Hal capsizes when sailing a small boat single-handed. He is rescued by Barry Gorman, the character who becomes his friend. The scene is central in plot significance; it fixes Hal's state of being at the time, to say nothing of its symbolic implications. Only to have described the capsize would have been to throw all the emphasis on plot, action, event. To leave contemplative recuperation till later in the story – till, say, that night in bed, when Hal could have remembered it all and thought about it – would have been against the nature of the story itself, and would have delayed the recuperation until after the reader had encountered other events, all of them depending for an understanding of their meaning on the reader's understanding of the meaning of the capsize.

Therefore, immediately after the description of the capsize there comes an 'Action Replay' in which Hal's memory is treated linguistically, as TV treats such a device visually. You read a slow-motion version with commentary. You contemplate the events even while being told what has happened.

Later on, the device of slow-motion is used again in the scene in which Hal is involved in a street brawl. (This is the companion scene to the moment in *Breaktime* in which Ditto is hit in the face, which is given the opposite treatment from Hal's: that is, fast-motion shown visually in a cartoon drawing and without commentary.) The focus of the scene is not the fight with the bikers, the what-happens-next action element of the plot, but the state of being in the fight. For me, the slowing down of the action and the camera angles, so to speak, used to show the events literally blow-by-blow, allow for commentary which fast-motion description hasn't time for, all contribute to making the scene comic and contemplative in nature rather than adventurously exciting in the instant-thrill manner.

I'm reminded of a remark I overheard after giving the lecture on which this chapter is based. A member of the audience turned to her companion and asked, 'Is all that really in the book?' Her companion replied, 'If you want it to be.'

I know I've mentioned contemplation a number of times. That's because, for me, all reading is an act of contemplation. Writing is simply a part of that ritual activity. I write that I may read, and so contemplate what I've written. Only in contemplation do I realise myself. Some will say this invests the reading of literature with spiritual significance. I wouldn't argue with that. For me, it has.

None of my writing, whether fictional or critical, is either an end in itself or ever comes to an end. None of it is self-contained. None of it is finished. All of it belongs, I hope and intend, to a continuum that cannot have an end. In other words, my intention is not merely to produce one book after another, but to create a body of work, each book of which belongs in one way and another to all the others.

References

This is an edited version of a lecture given at the University of Stockholm in May 1984 and published in *Booktalk*, The Bodley Head, 1985, now available from Thimble Press.

Roland Barthes, *Image-Music-Text*, Selected and translated by
    Stephen Heath, Fontana Collins, 1977. Pages 157, 146, 87, 161.

Wayne C Booth, *The Rhetoric of Fiction*, University of Chicago Press, 1961, 1983

Lewis Carroll, *Alice's Adventures in Wonderland and Through the Looking-Glass and What Alice Found There* (1871), ed. Peter Hunt, Oxford World's Classics, 2009. Pages 167-8.

Hans-Georg Gadamer, *Truth and Method*, trans. William Glen-Doepel, ed. John Cumming & Garrett Barden, Sheed & Ward (1975), 1979. Page 264.

Gérard Genette, *Narrative Discourse*, trans. Jane E. Lewin, Basil Blackwell, 1980. Pages 26-7, 29.

Alvin Kernan, *The Revels History of Drama in English*, Volume III 1560-1613. Methuen, 1975. Page 308.

Viktor Shklovsky, *The Theory of Prose*, trans. Benjamin Sher, Dalkey Archive Press (1990), 1991. Page 20.

CLOSURE

CHAPTER 14
AND NOW?

At the heart of these reflections is the question: Is youth fiction a literature in its own right or not? By now it must be clear that I think it is. That it is not accepted is obvious. Why is this so?

Because youth fiction is commonly thought of as being meant only for youth readers, the life of each book depends on its popularity with them. But instant gratification is short-lived and fashions in youthhood taste are notoriously fickle, so an inbuilt ephemerality goes along with the very idea of youth fiction.

And because youth fiction is regarded as for youth readers, those who are seriously interested in it tend to be professionals, like teachers and librarians, who concentrate on it not as a literature but on critical approaches such as reader reception, popular and populist fiction, sociological, bibliotherapeutic, educational and other uses.

The result is that the training of teachers and librarians and even academic students mainly concentrates on current books, and on newly published books that might interest youth readers. The discussions often focus on such topics as genre, ethnic and other sociological and political diversities. With few exceptions, the history of youth fiction isn't studied. Books from the past are not read because youth readers don't read them. Which means there is no depth of knowledge or understanding of the books as literature.

Think of what, for want of a better expression, I'll call 'adult literature'. No one seriously interested in it suggests that only fiction should be studied which has been published recently and provides instant gratification to a large number of the generality of readers. For example, in 'best seller' judgement, how many people today read James Joyce's *Ulysses* and *Finnegans Wake*, Robert Musil's *The Man Without Qualities*, Valeria Luiselli's *Faces in the Crowd*, and Vasily Grossman's *Life and Fate*? How widely popular are the stories of Mary Shelley, William Faulkner, Edith Wharton, Gertrude Stein, Samuel Beckett, Willa Cather, Franz Kafka, Marguerite Duras, Clarice Lispector, Robert Walser, Italo Calvino, and Lydia Davis? Or, come to that, the work of Marcel Proust, George Eliot or Laurence Sterne? Would anyone seriously suggest it is not necessary for students to be aware of *The Canterbury Tales*, *Don Quixote*, *Clarissa*, *Candide*, *Madame Bovary*, *The Sufferings of Young Werther*, *Moby Dick*, *The Awkward Age*? Each of these is a spur-of-the-moment choice from the accepted canon.

Which leads to the point that fiction is only studied as a literature if there is a canon – a list or lists of books it is generally agreed serious students should at least know about, if not read. Of course, there is constant argument about which books the canon should include, but it provides a grounding. And there are what might be called sub-canons – lists particular to a group of readers who have a special interest in one aspect of the literature. Eighteenth-century novels, for example, or novels written by women.

Until the history of youth fiction is studied; until there is a canon or canons to provide a grounding; until books are read because they are significant in the history of youth fiction, regardless of whether these are read now, youth fiction can be nothing more than an amorphous product supplied by commercial publishers in order to make money by satisfying a market, whether of youth readers themselves or those who promote the books, such as teachers, librarians and parents.

My experience as a writer of youth fictions has taken me on the journey from writing for youth readers to authoring fictions as works of art. Along the way this has meant giving the same attention to youth fiction as is given to the books accepted and studied as literary in the 'adult' field.

In these reflections I've tried to indicate some of the lessons I've learned.

What should happen now, if youth fiction is to be treated as a separate literature with a poetics of its own? We need a canon. We need to encourage interest in the fiction from which youth fiction evolved, and those books from the past which are significant and innovative as literary and formative examples. We need to stop regarding youth fiction as only for the immediate gratification of youth readers or merely as a tool for other purposes. We need to work out the poetics and the aesthetics of it. We need to appreciate it for its own sake, for what it is and can be as a particular artform.

As for myself, at eighty-five I'm still as strongly impelled to face the blank page every day and fill it with words composed in stories as I was when I was fifteen and the obsessive compulsion inexplicably took hold. And, to adapt the words of the greatest author of us all, I am more than ever aware that I am myself composed only of such stuff as dreams are made on, and my little life will soon be rounded with a sleep.

CHAPTER 15
AN INTERVIEW

After reading the chapters of *The Age Between*, Dr Deborah Cogan Thacker, university lecturer and academic with a special interest in children's, youth literature and literary theory, interviewed the author.

FINDING THE VOICE

Debby: You make a distinction [in your book here] between youth being observed and youth observing itself. Do you make that distinction [during] the process of writing?

Aidan: I do make the distinction, as a feature of youth literature. But for me, when writing a story, everything depends on the characters and their stories. The stories determine what happens. Everything to do with why the events in the story happen, what is thought and felt about them, what is done because of them and why, and how other [characters] behave is determined by the focalising youth characters. There are times in a story when one character observes another. But then, what they describe is written in their voice and from their point of view.

It's true that on an off day, I find myself writing a scene which isn't determined by the narrating youth character, but by myself. It happens when I'm not for that moment inhabited by his or her character. At those times, it feels as if the youth character has gone to sleep. I know, then, that the only thing to do is wait till he or she wakes up again and continues to tell the story. This must sound like potted psychology or pseudo-mystical. I don't mean it to be. But I can't think of any other way to express it. Certainly, when the writing is going well I do feel as if the character is inhabiting me. Or, to put it another away, perhaps more accurately, it's as if I've become the character. I think that's why I spend so much time preparing to write a novel – three, four, five years; longer for *Dance on My Grave* and *Postcards from No Man's Land*. I have to know as much as possible about the characters and their stories, and give them time to come alive in me, and, so to speak, take me over. Only when I'm thinking and feeling, and seeing the world and other people as the characters do, can I begin writing 'as them'. I've read that some writers feel like the character is dictating the story to them. That's not how I feel. I feel as if I am the character.

Debby: This makes me think about what Roland Barthes says in *The Preparation of the Novel*: '*I write and in doing so I am affected*; I make myself the center and the agent of the action; I establish myself in the action, not by adopting an external position (like the priest) but an internal one, where the subject and the action form one and the same bubble.' [Emphasis in the original.]

Aidan: That's exactly what I feel. I'm a huge fan of Roland Barthes. He's not just a literary critic, he's a great artist. He's turned literary criticism into an artform as important as the literature he writes about. Think of *S/Z* for example. *The Preparation of the Novel*, which was his last book, is by far and away the best book I've ever read on what it means to write a novel, how it's done, and what the author does. (I'd make it required reading in all creative writing courses.) It's composed of his lecture notes for a long course and seminars at the Collège de France between 1978 and 1980. It makes lecture notes into an artwork. I wish I'd had this book when I set out to be a writer of novels, because it would have helped me more than anything or anyone else has – and would have saved me a lot of time and anguish!

Debby: Do you think there are any particular reasons

that the characters you become are of the age between?

Aidan: I've often wondered about this and don't have a clear answer. I don't think it's entirely due to the fact that I became a published writer by writing *for* the age between. I suppose it would need a psychologist to dig out the reasons. But one reason might be how much my life changed during my middle to late teenage years. It changed culturally, educationally, intellectually, and even geographically – the change began when we moved from a row of houses all by themselves in the country outside Chester-le-Street in the north of England to the large town of Darlington. A change from rural to urban, secluded to crowded, agricultural to industrial, badly, in fact appallingly educated to much better educated, and becoming a passionate reader. Not to mention all the changes that go on in everyone at that time of life.

Debby: I wonder whether you feel the characters 'choose' to come to you, or whether you determine that these are youths in some way.

Aidan: I don't feel they choose me and I don't set out by deciding I'll write about youth characters. That's determined by the story, which comes to me 'out of the blue', so to speak. Readers often ask where I get my ideas from. The answer is that they come from anywhere and usually take me by surprise. *Dance on My Grave* came to me when I read a newspaper report about a sixteen-year-old boy who had been charged with desecrating a grave. *Now I Know* began with those words, used in a seminal scene in Milan Kundera's novel *The Book of Laughter and Forgetting*, the initials of which spell Nik, which I knew at once must be the name of the central character. *The Toll Bridge* began when I was travelling to Oxford once a week during the 1980s and drove over a toll bridge where the money was taken by the same man, dressed summer and winter in the same old clothes, and I wondered who he was and how he came to do such a boring job.

Debby: I know that you admire the work of Philip Roth. In his *Paris Review* interview, he talks about being a ventriloquist. His art consists of him being present and absent. From what you say, that isn't true for you?

Aidan: Roth's *PR* interview is fascinating and full of important thoughts about writing novels. But, no, I don't feel like a ventriloquist. But I do understand what he means by being present and absent when writing. In a sense you're two people at the same time. You're the self who is the author, observing what you are writing, and at the same time you're the self who is the narrator, whether that is a first-person protagonist, as in so many of Roth's novels, or is a third-person narrator who is an unknown presence outside the story. To give an example, I was both Hal, who narrates his story in *Dance on My Grave*, and at the same time I was a forty-year-old adult monitoring what Hal had written. I might express this as Hal being the creator of the story and the adult me acting as his editor and first reader, helping to refine and hone what he had written.

Debby: How does that work in the process of writing?

Aidan: There comes a day when preparing a novel that I feel strongly it's time to start writing the story. At that moment, I scribble as fast as I can whatever opening sentences come into my head. I let this alone for a day or two. Then, until 1984 I typed them, double-spaced, and since 1984 I've typed them onto an A5 format that is as much like the page in a book typographically as I can make it. I leave this alone for a day, then read it. It's almost always wrong, and I lose confidence. I wait until I've recovered my confidence, then try again. This process continues, sometimes with long gaps between attempts, until I've found the narrative voice that feels right. Only then can I settle down to write the book. To be clear, I should explain that when drafting a scene I'm the character writing it. Afterwards, when I type it, I'm my writer-self, revising the text, honing it for rhythm, language, structure, shape and pace.

Debby: I think it's very interesting that you sustain such distinctive voices, down to the flow of speech, a particular sense of humour, etc. As with Huck, there's a thinking process in the first-person that you create for the characters, such as Piers/Jan in *The Toll Bridge*. And each character is distinct from the others, so that Adam and Tess have different language and rhythms.

Aidan: You say there's a thinking process I create for the characters. But I don't create it, they do! And it's achieved only in the writing, not in the preparation before the writing starts. During the preparation, which, as I said, can take years, I'm finding out about the characters, rather as you might find out about someone you meet and who then becomes a loved friend. I want to know as much about them as possible. Knowing their names is an essential feature. Their family background. What they look like, how they move, dress, what food and music and other things they like and don't like, what they fantasise about, their opinions about their parents, friends, teachers, and so on.

Most important of all, is how they talk and how they think. But these only come alive as I write the story. They create themselves in the writing. And often the characters turn out to be different in the writing from what I thought they were during the preparation.

Debby: Can you give an example of when this happened?

Aidan: Barry in *Dance on My Grave* became a much more selfish and manipulative person than I'd expected. And I didn't expect that Julie in *Now I Know* would turn up again twenty years later in *This Is All*. I thought the character was only Cordelia's teacher. Didn't have a name for her; couldn't find the one that seemed right. It wasn't until I was writing the book and the first scene in which she appears that her name occurred to me as if waiting for me, and I realised who she was. And what had happened to her in the twenty years since she was a nineteen-year-old. Which added richness to the character, and Cordelia's story. It was, in fact, for me, a turning point in the composition of the book.

Debby: So the characters grow and develop and are

changed by the events that happen to them in their stories?

Aidan: Yes, just as we all are by the events of our lives. And I only find this out while writing the stories. You mention the distinctly different voices of each of the characters in a story. Achieving this creates a problem. If there's a passage – a section or a chapter, for example – in the voice of one of the characters followed by a passage in the voice of one of the other characters, I can't write both passages on the same day. I need time overnight to keep the two voices separate and strong in my imagination.

Debby: I know you love theatre and as a teenager wanted to work in theatre. I think I'm right in saying you've directed over fifteen amateur productions, mostly with young actors. Your first published books were plays, and you've written for both TV and radio. Is there an aspect of that background that influences the way you write novels and short stories?

Aidan: Yes, there is. When writing a story I see it in my imagination as if it were a play or a film. And when writing I'm 'performing' the characters. *Dance on My Grave*, for example, is almost a film script in many ways. I'm delighted to say that the French director, François Ozon, has made a film adaptation called *Summer of 85* (*Été 85*). It has also been produced as a stage play three times now – in Flanders and Germany, but never I'm sorry to say, in Britain. And there have been stage adaptations of *Breaktime*, *The Toll Bridge*, and *This Is All* in the Netherlands and Flanders.

Debby: Does what you read influence your writing? How do you decide what to read?

Aidan: I read all the time. To be frank, I much prefer reading to writing. When I'm working solidly at a book I have to be careful what I read. It's too easy to be influenced. In style, say, or form. [The decision is] instinctive. It's a bit like knowing what food you'd like to eat for a meal. I'll start reading and know very quickly that this will get in the way, so to speak. It isn't what I need at that moment. Or it will be helpful. Often what I need is information that will help me write a scene. As for example, finding Paffard's *Inglorious Wordsworths* about young people's epiphanies, just when I needed it while composing *Now I Know*. Also, some books make me want to write and some put me off. For example, when I was writing *The Toll Bridge* I read Iris Murdoch's novels all the time. I can't explain why. And of course, *The Pillow Book* by Sei Shōnagon was both an inspiration and a model for *This Is All*.

Debby: I've forgotten who it was, who said that they write either because they feel they can do better than some writers they read or because they admired a writer's work so much they wanted to emulate it. Is that true for you?

Aidan: Yes, to some extent it is. Both stimulate me to keep writing, even when I know I can't be as good as the authors I admire most. Also, I know it's true that I couldn't write if I didn't read. For me, reading is the great redeemer, the greatest encouragement, provides me with models and exemplars, and gives me the greatest pleasure.

DEPICTION OF ADULT CHARACTERS IN YOUTH FICTIONS

Debby: One of the familiar tropes of youth fiction, particularly at the 'popular' end, is the rejection of adult values. There are very few laudable adult characters in youth fiction, generally. For Salinger, they are all phonies, for Twain, they are tainted (except for Jim, who shows himself to be childlike and a loving father). There isn't really anyone in *The Chocolate War*, either. But your novels often celebrate the sympathetic adult. And they are often teachers; Midgely in *Breaktime*, Osborn in *Dance*, and Julie in *This Is All*. Why do you think this is?

Aidan: I've always felt uncomfortable with the negative treatment of adults in a lot of youth fiction. It's one of the reasons I'm uneasy about *Catcher*. It just isn't true to life. Yes, I know, there are times when teenagers find adults, especially their parents, boring or wrong or annoying or out of date. But that's not how most of them feel all the time. Indeed, for most youths, there are adults they like, admire, respect, and imitate, and I'll add love. That's how it was for me, and it's how it is for the vast majority of young people I've observed throughout my life. Which is why I've tried to present this aspect of youthhood in my novels.

You mention that the sympathetic adults in my novels are often teachers. Perhaps that's because of my experience as a youth and as a teacher. But in my own defence, I'll mention Ditto's mother in *Breaktime*, the social worker in *Dance*, Nik's grandfather in *Now I Know*, Tess's father and Jan's father and the doctor in *The Toll Bridge*, Alma, Geertrui, Daan's mother, and Jacob's grandmother in *Postcards*, William's father, and Cordelia's father and her aunt Doris in *This Is All*. Not to mention the unnamed adult narrator of *Dying to Know You*. There are others. All sympathetic and I hope convincingly real. Not such a short list, and more than the number of sympathetic teachers.

Debby: I suppose it might be more helpful, then, to think about what all of these adults have in common (if they do). Would you say that it's an attitude to youthhood? Memories of (as distinct from nostalgia for) their own youths? Respect for young people?

Aidan: I have to admit I've never thought of them like that. Thinking about it now, I'd say it depends on their own nature and their relationship with the young person. Most of them are either family members or they have a professional relationship as teachers or a social worker, which means they naturally have a regard for the young people they are involved with. But there are exceptions. For example, Hal's father is very unsympathetic, indeed domineering and aggressive; mainly, I think, because he doesn't understand his son and doesn't know what to do about him. Hal isn't the son he wanted. The careers teacher at Hal's school doesn't like him for reasons she makes all too plain. William's mother in

This Is All is harsh in her treatment of Cordelia because she thinks Cordelia isn't good enough for her son. In each case the relationship is a matter of the character's own nature and their attitude to the younger person. So again, I suppose what I'm saying is that everything is determined by the story and what happens, to whom, and why.

IMPLIED READER & READER-IN-THE-BOOK

Debby: This makes me wonder how you think about your 'implied reader', the concept you wrote about in your widely read essay 'The Reader in the Book', first published in *Signal 23* in May 1977.

Aidan: Reading Wolfgang Iser's *The Implied Reader* was a turning point in my writing. I was working on *Breaktime*, which I began in 1975, and struggling with the question 'Who am I writing this for?' Till then, as I explain in the first chapter of this book, I had written for the pupils I taught in the 1960s, who were mostly either non-readers of fiction or reluctant. I began writing *Breaktime* without any preparation, letting the story compose itself day by day, scene by scene. From the beginning, the story was told by Ditto, the youthhood protagonist, to his friend, Morgan, who is therefore the reader-in-the-book. I didn't decide this beforehand, it simply started that way. I still thought of myself as a writer who would be read by teenagers. Perhaps I unconsciously knew I needed an implied reader who would represent the flesh-and-blood reader I hoped would read the novel. Iser's book helped me understand what I was doing and why.

Debby: But isn't that more of a challenge when you are more mature and knowledgeable than your implied reader?

Aidan: I haven't found that to be the case. Until recently my memory of my teenage years has always been very vivid, very alive. After reading Iser I found it fairly easy to identify the implied reader in most fiction. But as an author I've found it difficult. As a critical reader, you're dealing with a finished story. All the evidence you need to identify the implied reader is in the text. But as an author you're starting from scratch. You're the one creating the evidence.

In most of my youth fiction since 1975 I've solved the problem by including a character who is the reader the narrator is addressing. In *Breaktime* it's Morgan. In *Dance on My Grave* it's the social worker Ms Atkins. In *The Toll Bridge* the reader-in-the-book is meant to be Adam when he has recovered from his fugue state. In *This Is All* it's Cordelia's daughter when she is sixteen. The novel in this sequence which is entirely without a character to whom the story is addressed is *Postcards*. That's because the youthful central character Jacob is himself the implied reader. He's writing his story as a way of helping himself understand what has happened to him and why. He uses the third person because he's writing the story soon after it has happened (when he has returned home) and wants to distance himself from the immediacy of the experiences so that he can think about them reflectively and 'coolly'. This isn't stated in the text. But it was my intention while writing the story, and this determined everything told in the story.

Debby: You haven't mentioned *Now I Know*, which is the third in the Dance Sequence of six novels.

Aidan: Because *Now I Know* is more complex in this regard. Mostly the reader-in-the-book is meant to be Julie – or Nik when Julie writes letters to him. But there are passages, such as the opening, when neither seems to be the implied reader. One reason for this is that I wanted to include a point of view from a mature adult perspective. I was trying to expand the range of insights, the variety of ways of seeing and thinking about the story and what was happening to the characters and how they were reacting. *Now I Know* has sometimes been called the most difficult of the six novels to read, and perhaps that's why.

Debby: It's clear that this aspect of writing – the attention you pay to the reader – is central to the way you talk about your own work. Is there anything about your history as a reader that influences your view of your implied reader?

Aidan: Now you mention it, I think there is. As you know, I couldn't read fluently until I was nine, and didn't become a serious reader till I was about fourteen. And then only with the help and influence of a brilliant teacher, Jim Osborn, to whom I owe more than I dare say. I'm also a very slow reader. I have to hear every word in my head as if it's being read aloud. Not only that, but also I have a short concentration span. This means I prefer books composed of short chapters or which are broken up into small units.

Another factor: my years teaching young people who weren't enthusiastic readers, and who liked short books – the readers I began my career writing for – have perhaps also conditioned my view of the implied reader of the fiction I write. I suppose it's for those reasons that all my novels are composed of short passages, often numbered or titled, often no longer than three or four pages at most. It suits me, feels natural. I don't think about it when I'm writing. The story grows that way of its own accord.

In his superb book *Six Memos for the Next Millennium*, the great Italian author Italo Calvino suggested that in the twenty-first century literature would be written in very short passages contained in very long books. I like that. It exactly describes what I prefer to read and to write. For instance, the novel I think is my best and most successful – by which I mean it comes closest to the original concept of the book – is *This Is All*. It's the longest I've written and is mainly composed of short passages of many different kinds. Exactly the kind of novel I like to read!

READER RESPONSE

Debby: This reminds me that you've spoken about responses from some of your readers and how they tell you that they like your novels because they make them think.

How do you make this work?

Aidan: I'm happy to be told this. But of course, you can't make people think! I want them to think and would like to help them to. Wittgenstein says what I mean better than I can: 'I should not like my writing to spare other people the trouble of thinking. But, if possible, to stimulate someone to thoughts of their own.' I have to come back again to what I said earlier. Everything depends on the story and the characters. It has often been remarked by reviewers and critics, not always intended as a compliment, that my stories are about characters who think a lot, and read, and often write, and that most teenagers are not like that.

Debby: Yes, your characters think a lot and that is one of the things that makes your work distinct. Are these thoughts you think (or have thought as a 'youth')?

Aidan: They are the thoughts the characters have. To start with, I don't believe it's true that most teenagers don't think or aren't interested in thinking, but only in emotions. Quite the contrary. My experience of talking to teenaged readers is that they very much enjoy and welcome the chance to think about all sorts of subjects and about what they've read. I was certainly like that myself in my youth.

That said, whether right or wrong, I suppose the readers who like my novels feel companionship with the characters. So much so that they often talk about the characters as if they were real and not fictions. I remember an email from a teenaged Swedish girl who had read *Postcards from No Man's Land*. She said she loved Jacob and his story so much she wanted to go to Amsterdam and see the places that Jacob sees and meet him! She added that she knew Jacob wasn't a real person, but she still felt she could meet him in Amsterdam. This is particularly true of *This Is All*, which receives very passionate responses.

I understand what the Swedish girl meant. I had the same experience at the age of fifteen when I first read D. H. Lawrence's *Sons and Lovers*. I felt I was Paul Morel, because his life was so like mine. I knew of course that I wasn't him and he wasn't real, but at the same time he felt more real, more there beside me, and that I knew him better than any of my real-life friends and schoolmates.

By the way, it was reading this book which shifted me into being an independent, self-determined, confident reader rather than only a student reader guided by my teacher Jim Osborn.

READING AS COMPANIONSHIP

Debby: What do you look for when you read? Is it the narrative voice that you connect with?

Aidan: What I look for is a consciousness that I want to spend time with. It's the personality of the author-in-the-book. Some people call this the author's second self. I think about it like this: Reading is about companionship. Wayne C. Booth's *The Company We Keep* is an extensive discussion of that reality. I'm sure I'm not alone in feeling that the books, the authors, that matter most to me, the ones I keep near me and reread, are friends who enliven me, refresh and clarify my thoughts and my use of language, focus my mind, amuse and move me, and speak better for me what I cannot speak so well by myself.

There's another way of describing one of the things I look for as a reader, and try to do in my novels, and is an example of an author saying for me what I cannot say so well myself. It comes from *The Sufferings of Young Werther* by Goethe, a precursor of youth fiction: 'And I do love best of all that author in whom I rediscover my own world, in whose books things happen the way they do all around me, and whose story is as interesting and heartfelt as my own domestic life, which, of course, is no paradise and yet all in all is a source of inexpressible happiness.'

Debby: So, are you trying to change the world?

Aidan: Not at all! I hope I have enough sense to know I'd fail if I tried. All I'm trying to do is describe the world as I and my characters perceive it. And trying to make sense of it. Very often when composing a scene, I find myself writing thoughts I've never had before and didn't know I knew, but which the character who is inhabiting me knows and causes me to write. It's a very strange feeling when this happens. And it isn't peculiar to me. I've heard other writers describe it too.

MULTIPLE PERSONALITIES

Debby: I came across this passage in *The Toll Bridge*: The doctor says, 'We coexist as our selves. We are multiple beings. A mix of actualities and potentialities. One of the many things the so-called mentally ill have taught me is that we so-called healthy people are not very good at exploring our possible selves. Perhaps because we feel reasonably happy with the selves we are living. But perhaps we are the most imprisoned of all because of that. Whereas the mentally ill, being uncomfortable with their actual selves, sometimes explore their potentialities and find selves they like better and try them out.' First of all, I wondered whether this was a particularly significant thing to say in a novel for young people, in terms of their position in thinking about their selves.

Aidan: I do believe this is a significant thing to deal with in a youth novel, because 'exploring your potentialities' and discovering who you are and your many different selves is central to youthhood experience. But I don't think you need to be mentally ill to do it! Though perhaps we all need help to do it. For me, the best help is through fictional accounts of characters doing it.

Debby: I wondered whether this is what fiction allows; finding different selves and trying them out?

Aidan: I'm very interested in the different selves we are and can be and how in fiction we can try them out. Milan Kundera said that 'A novel is a meditation on existence seen through imaginary characters.' George Eliot said that 'Art is the nearest thing to life; it is a mode of amplifying experience with our fellow-men beyond the bounds of our personal lot.' In *Culture and Value* Ludwig Wittgenstein said, 'Nothing is more important for teaching us to understand the concepts we have than constructing fictitious ones.' For me, my novels are meditations. And I hope they are modes of amplifying experience, and are attempts to understand who and what we are.

ETHICS, MORALITY & RESPONSIBILITY

Debby: How do you balance the responsibility of writing about the age between, knowing you want readers of that age to read your novels, indeed, perhaps being your primary readership, as against the subject matter that often preoccupies that age?

Aidan: Your question assumes the writer owes a responsibility to his youth readers, because they are not yet fully mature adults. That begs the question whether a writer owes a responsibility to readers whatever their age. I'm reminded of a class of children in a primary school who had read my children's novel *The Present Takers*. I was invited to talk to them about the book. The subject of responsibility came up. Was Melanie, the bully in the story, responsible for what she did or not? Were the teachers responsible for not having noticed what was going on and dealing with it? And Lucy's parents, who knew what was going on? The class talked very well about this, arguing the pros and cons, the whys and wherefores. At one point I asked them if they thought I, as the author, had any responsibility to them as readers? One of the boys said, 'Your responsibility is to write the best book you can.' That sums it up very well. But I've tussled with the complexities of the question of the ethics and morals of writing novels, and have never resolved it to my own satisfaction.

Debby: Are there ethical considerations?

Aidan: In principle, I believe that one of the functions of literature is to deal with all aspects of life. Not of course in every book, but overall. For me, what defines youth fiction is that it deals with life from the perspective of youthhood. When I started writing *Breaktime*, I set myself three morally determined guides.

First, the story could include anything that the youthhood characters could do, witness, or hear about in real life, whatever the current moral attitude. Second, I would not compromise on language. It's my belief – and experience with them – that people in the age between are as capable as I am of understanding and using language, if they want to, and are as capable as I am of looking up what unfamiliar words and phrases and references mean. Third, I would make no concession to the formal aspects of the story – the ways of telling it, no matter how complicated or different from the straightforward narrative that is conventional and usual in youth fiction.

Debby: Is there anything you wouldn't put into a novel, even if it is something a young person could experience or observe in reality?

Aidan: Yes, there is. But not because of any moral or ethical reason. [For example] I detest hard-core drug taking. I think it's profoundly destructive, not only of the people who do it, but of society as a whole. I've witnessed it, which means I could describe it. But my judgemental attitude would warp my relation to the characters involved, and the telling of the scene. In other words, the story would become infected with a dogmatic statement.

Debby: But you could tell a story in which a central character felt as you do.

Aidan: I could. But I don't want to. Other writers deal with that aspect of life.

Debby: Do you see that as a responsibility?

Aidan: Yes. To myself. To the artform. And to readers. It would be dishonest of me to tackle the subject in the form of a novel, as against an essay or an article in a journal.

RELATIVITY & MULTIPLE POINTS OF VIEW

Debby: Is that part of the reason why your books so often contain multiple voices and shifts in narrative from one chapter to the next (or, as in *Breaktime*, three simultaneous narratives)? What inspired you to do this?

Aidan: With *Breaktime* the influence was the modernist novels of B.S. Johnson, such as *Albert Angelo* and *Christie Malry's Own Double-Entry*. Later, when I was working on *Dance*, reading Roland Barthes helped me understand relativity as the reason for the multiple voices. This is a particular feature of twentieth-century literature. Think not only of Italo Calvino but even more of James Joyce's *Ulysses*, for example, and Virginia Woolf's *To the Lighthouse* and *The Waves*. We know that no one's account of an event is definitive. No one's view of life is the complete truth. I'm reminded of how this point is amusingly made in Raymond Queneau's *Exercises in Style* [*Exercises de Style*] in which a brawl on a Paris bus is told in 99 different ways, as seen by 99 different people. Sometimes we still tell stories only from the point of view of one character, as Salinger does in *Catcher*. Sometimes we tell stories which include more than one character's point of view of the same incidents, as Robert Cormier does in *The Chocolate War* and as I do in *The Toll Bridge*.

The scene you mention in *Breaktime* includes three different points of view within the same character. There are relativities even inside us about ourselves!

I like to include at some point in a novel a different point of view from the predominant one. For example, in *Dance*, here and there in the story we read the reports of her meetings with Hal by the social worker, Ms Atkins, for whom Hal is writing his account of what happened between him and Barry. In this way we see him through someone else's eyes rather than only seeing him through his own eyes. The most subtle and complex of my novels in this respect is *This Is All*. In the chapters 'How to do more with the First Person' and 'Ways of Telling' I try to explain how other points of view can be included in a first-person narrative.

Debby: Do such complex narratives set too high a bar for your young readers?

Aidan: Not in my opinion. It's my experience that people in the age between are as capable as I am of reading unfamiliar forms of narrative, and that many of them like doing so. What I try to do is to engage their interest from the start of the book. The first pages are vital for capturing a reader's interest. Which is why I spend a long time getting them right. I mean 'right' in the sense that they indicate the kind of novel this is, the ways in which the story will be told, and the kind of linguistic and other demands it will make on the reader. I don't mean I pander to the reader by starting the story with some easy, sensational, catchy opening. Rather, I'm saying: Look, this is what this story is like, what it's about, and the kind of reading it needs. If you don't like it, don't waste your time by reading any further.

Debby: This makes me think about the concept of defamiliarisation (*ostrananie*), in Viktor Shklovsky's sense, in 'Art as Technique': 'The purpose of art is to impart the sensation of things as they are perceived and not as they are known. The technique of art, then, is to lead us to a knowledge of a thing through the organ of sight instead of recognition. By "enstranging" objects and complicating form, the device of art makes perception long and "laborious." The perceptual process in art has a purpose all its own and ought to be extended to the fullest. *Art is a means of experiencing the process of creativity. The artefact itself is quite unimportant.*' [Emphasis in original] The invitations into your books often enstrange, or, as it is sometimes translated, defamiliarise the process of reading – the reader becomes aware of both the reading and writing process – so that what is taken for granted in the reading process is exposed by the challenges you set your readers. Does this make sense?

Aidan: Yes, it does. I don't mean I make things difficult just for the sake of making them difficult. But when you tell a story in ways that are different from those a reader is familiar with, the reader is bound to find it a bit difficult at first. And because this is the case children and youths often need the help of someone who enables them to understand and be interested in the difficulty. For most of us this person is a teacher. For those born into homes where serious reading is normal, the help can come from parents, relatives, friends.

SUCCESS OR FAILURE?

Debby: How do you judge the success of your novels?

Aidan: By how closely they come to the original concept I had in my imagination. Certainly, I don't judge their success by how many readers they gain. I'm not in the populist business (and it is a business) of producing bestsellers. I'm trying to make an object, which – let's use the right word – is an artwork. When the novel is published, of course, I'm interested in who reads it and why and how many. But that isn't anything I think about while writing. And whatever is said afterwards has no influence on what I write next. In any case, by the time a novel is published, I'm already well into preparations for the next book.

Debby: If you were writing the same novel 'for adults', would you write it differently? [And if so] is it about age, or is it the receptivity of the reader to the kind of reading that you offer that comes into play?

Aidan: It's about point of view and the implied reader. I'd assume a much wider and deeper knowledge of life and of possible references than I can assume in a youth reader. And I would be much less concerned about the formative moral impact of the story. By which I mean, you cannot escape the fact that youth readers are by definition not yet mature adults. Therefore, they are still forming their understanding of themselves and of life in general. And the author has a responsibility to keep this in mind.

PREPARATION & RESEARCH

Debby: What kind of research do you do to prepare?

Aidan: You can see from the chapter 'Ways of Telling' how I plan the structure of a story. This grows out of a lot of what people call research. For me this means finding out what I need to know – information – required by the plot and the thematic material. For example, in *Postcards* I needed to know everything I could about the Battle of Arnhem (the famous battle for the 'bridge too far'). There are several books about this, some are academic accounts, some are personal reminiscences by soldiers and local people who were involved. But that wasn't enough. I needed to see where it happened. So I went twice to Arnhem and Oosterbeek, outside Arnhem, both places where the battle took place. Once was for the annual memorial commemoration held in the allied cemetery at Oosterbeek, because this was a scene I knew would be in the book.

Debby: When do you decide you need to know more?

Aidan: A difficult question to answer briefly. It has to do with the way the plot develops. The first idea – the first conception of the story – gets me started. With *Postcards* I knew from the beginning certain things were involved. For example, it would happen in a foreign country where English was well understood and spoken. A battle in the Second World War would come into it. And a city. (Forgive me if I don't explain how I knew these were essential; it has to do with the novel's relation to the other five in the Dance Sequence.) When I looked for a country and places in it where all these features were available Holland, Amsterdam, and the Battle of Arnhem came to mind fairly quickly because I already knew [those places] from frequent visits. And the

Battle of Arnhem was useful because it was self-contained. It happened over a period of a few days in that one place. I wouldn't have to explain more about the context of the battle in order for readers to understand what was happening.

Once I've found those major features, others come into view. For example, Anne Frank lived and wrote her diary in Amsterdam during the Second World War. I'd always loved her *Diary* and her. Rembrandt lived and worked in Amsterdam; I knew his paintings and regard him as one of the greatest painters ever. I didn't know how they might, but was sure these could give me more layers of significant meaning. I'd visited the Frank house and thought Jacob, the developing central character of the story, would also visit the house, because everybody, especially young people, who go to Amsterdam does. Similarly, I'd spent hours looking at Rembrandt's paintings in the Rijksmuseum. But I didn't know till I started writing the story how they would fit in and relate to the other events, the characters, and the various themes.

Debby: Writers sometimes talk about the importance (and difficulty) of finding the right beginning. Is that true for you?

Aidan: It is. I usually try many openings before I find the right one. For example, the opening of *Postcards* came to me when my Dutch friend Mance Post, who had been a teenager during the German occupation of Amsterdam, told me about a boy she had come across recently who had been mugged, losing all his money and passport, and was sitting in distress on the steps beside her basement apartment when she came across him. And being Mance, one of the most generous and compassionate people I have ever met, she helped him with money and put him in touch with people who he knew. As soon as she told me this episode I knew it would be perfect for the start of my novel.

Also, Mance told me a lot about what life was like during the German occupation. And I used her as the model for Alma and her basement apartment. In fact, all the names I used for the characters are taken from my Dutch friends. And all the places in the book are in Amsterdam and Oosterbeek near Arnhem. You could take the novel page by page and find your way round Amsterdam as if following a map. Which I know some readers have done, because they've told me!

So the story grows, the developing plot leading to information I need to find out and to locations for the story. This background work brings to mind incidents I've experienced or have heard about. It helps develop the characters. A gradual weaving together of information, incidents, ideas, thematic material, plot and characters, in the way I've described in the chapter 'Ways of Telling'.

Debby: A slow process?

Aidan: Yes. And it's the part of the work that I enjoy the most. Which means I tend to do far more 'research' than I need to. A great deal of it is never used. But, at the same time, I'm sure that the resulting novel is better for having all that unused material underpinning it, so to speak. The better the mulch, the better the crop. Besides, I never know what might come out of the research. In other words, I'm not researching all the time, only what I know I need to know, but I'm 'wool gathering', as I put it. Harvesting as much stuff as I can that might have anything to do with the story.

By the way, I make notes of all the research I do in notebooks. These are kept in my archive, housed at the Seven Stories institution in Newcastle upon Tyne, where accredited students and people who are seriously interested in my books can read them and discover everything that went into the writing of the novels.

Debby: What about humour? Many of your characters become real through their banter and wordplay and there are shared, private jokes. Does this come out of the character?

Aidan: It isn't planned. I don't make it up and then add it to the text. It tends to come from the characters, or the narrator, as I write. Sometimes it comes as I'm revising a passage. In other words, like everything else in my novels, it grows organically during the writing.

THE READER AS REWRITER AND CO-AUTHOR

Debby: When I read your novels as well as your critical writing, I see all sorts of parallels with Jean-Paul Sartre's book *Qu'est ce que la literature?* (*What is Literature?*) He is not differentiating between young and adult readers but, I suppose, inattentive readers and readers at their 'best'.

Aidan: That's an attractive distinction. I'd say I write for attentive readers whatever their age. To put it another way, I'm not interested in pastime reading, but in reading which is thoughtful and discriminating.

Debby: Is it in youth that we have the potential to discover this truth about reading fiction?

Aidan: I've observed very good teachers in infant and primary schools helping their pupils become attentive, thoughtful readers. My book *Tell Me* is intended to help in this educational work. But it is in youth that we 'take this over' and learn to be attentive readers for ourselves. The main point here is that all of us have to be educated into becoming attentive readers. And we learn how to do this, as we learn all our cultural life, from adults who know how to do it. I'm saying that we cannot separate youth fiction and youth reading from education. They are intricately bound together.

Debby: Would you say that we need to ensure that young people are exposed to the kind of fiction that invites this kind of reading?

Aidan: Yes, I would. As we mentioned earlier, readers – all readers, but especially children and youths – need the assistance of mature readers – teachers, parents, friends, whoever – to help them grow as thoughtful, discriminating, wide-ranging readers who enjoy the experience of discovering 'difficult' books and how to read them – the ones that are unfamiliar to them. Forgive me for adapting a famous quotation: Ask not what I want this book to do for me but what this book wants me to do with it.

Populist reading is about reading that which you already know you like and which you use for little more than relaxation and passing the time. Serious reading is about a deep engagement with the author, the book, and yourself as a thinking, feeling, perceptive and developing human being. My own experience is that I learned this and how to do it from a brilliant teacher, and all my life from friends who were ahead of me in this respect.

Debby: In the chapter 'Why Write?' Sartre says: 'all literary work is an appeal. To write is to make an appeal to the reader that he leads into the objective existence the revelation which I have undertaken by means of language. Thus, reading is a pact of generosity between author and reader. Each one trusts the other; each one counts on the other, demands of the other, as much as he demands of himself.'

Aidan: I agree with both statements. To my mind, literature is an appeal. I'd go further, I'd say it's a gift. It's a gift from the author to the reader, just as an attentive reading is a gift from the reader to the author. It is, as I said earlier, a mutually respectful companionship.

Debby: According to Sartre, when the reader recognises that reading is creation, there is a kind of joy – a deep pleasure. This, I think, is akin to Roland Barthes' *jouissance*.

Aidan: Yes, I think it is. As you know, I'm not as keen on Sartre as I am on Barthes. As I mentioned earlier, *The Preparation of the Novel* covers all these aspects of writing and reading.

Debby: When we were discussing the Barthes book the other day we found this: 'The Hope of Writing Hope. Especially that Time of reading and of jubilatory reading that occurs in Adolescence – but also throughout a Writer's life, where nothing is given, and Desire is constantly being reborn ... Every beautiful work, or even every impressive work, functions as a desired work, albeit one that's incomplete and as it were lost *because I didn't write it myself*; in order to recover that work, I have to rewrite it; to write is to want to rewrite: I want to actively add myself to something that's beautiful but that I lack, that I *require*.' [Italics in original]

Aidan: Isn't that terrific! So elegant and dense and true. Key words to do with authoring: Desire. Incomplete. I didn't write it myself. It was written, to use Barthes' words, by the 'stranger who is within me, the stranger I am to myself'. Paul Ricoeur elaborates on this in his wonderful book *Oneself as Another*. To write is to want to rewrite and to actively add oneself. That is what I require. The density of the passage is like a text for meditation. You can spend hours unpacking the possible meanings and what they mean to a literary author.

Debby: And don't you agree that to recover the work, one has to rewrite it oneself as a reader? [And] this is a powerful position for a young reader, who is in the midst of the journey away from powerlessness?

Aidan: Indeed! To become a serious attentive reader you have to understand that you are rewriting the work, recreating it along with the author ... In my experience, as I explained about myself, you become conscious of the power of readerly rewriting most potently in youth. I think this is what happens stunningly when young readers find their 'epiphany' book, as I did with *Sons and Lovers*.

THE CONNECTION BETWEEN READING AND WRITING, AND READER EDUCATION

Debby: It seems to me there is a strong connection between your writing on reading, and the way you call attention to acts of writing and reading in your novels, always telling us more about the characters and their 'journeys'. Your interest in theorists such as Eco and Barthes suggests that the codes requiring 'writerly' or 'open' engagement on the part of the reader are embedded in your own poetics. You give an invitation to your readers to enter into a relationship with you, as much as the characters, in order to 'go beyond', as Sartre puts it: 'The reader must invent them all in a continual exceeding of the written thing. To be sure, the author guides him, but all he does is guide him ... In short, reading is a directed creation.'

Aidan: You're right. I've always been aware of the connection between writing and reading in my novels.

Debby: Is it a feature of youth fiction that the adult author guides the reader to a position where they can take up the invitation? Sartre considers that flattery is part of the process, and even the notion that there is a specific literature for 'young adults' could be seen as a kind of flattery.

Aidan: I have to agree that the author does guide the reader, though I'm not sure I'd call it flattery. Rather, an invitation to keep me company. But I think this applies to all writing. The appeal of youth fiction, however, is different in that it is to do with exceptionalism. Youth likes to think of itself as exceptional: different from either childhood or adulthood. And youth fiction includes that notion of being exceptional, or being different (think of Holden Caulfield in *Catcher*), not so much as belonging to the generality of people in the age between but as separate, unique individuals.

Perhaps in my writing this goes back to my own youth. I never, even as a child, wanted to belong to any group, whether of my peers or family, or any other category. I am by nature a solitary, an outsider. I always wanted, and still do, to be myself alone, making my own decisions about who I associate with and belong to. I once told a good friend that I have no family. He said I did. That I compose it of people I love and trust and feel at home with. He was right! And looking back, I see that this desire, this aim, this requirement of close, loving friendship, imbues all my fiction.

Debby: Do you think there are parallels with your *Tell Me* approach to booktalk? I was thinking of an attitude to your reader, or to readers in general, founded on respect for them as part of the creative process and the feeling of pleasure that this creates. In *Tell Me* you say: 'it is wiser, at least where booktalk is concerned, to act on the assumption that children are potentially all that we are ourselves and that in telling their own stories and their reading of other people's stories that "talk themselves into being". In telling their reading they activate their potentialities, but only when that reading is truly their own ... and is not someone else's reading imposed on them.'

I realise that there are key differences: the children talk, and the reader is silently reading, yet the thinking process, the realisation that meaning-making is dependent on them and the deep pleasure arising from that process, are common to both. I think this is what Sartre and Barthes are talking about, too.

Aidan: I heartily agree. I've always believed that the best teaching and the best writing respects the learner and the reader. I learned this early in my life, because the teacher who 'saved' me, Jim Osborn, always respected his pupils and encouraged them to say what they thought rather than repeat what they thought they were meant to say – always expecting them to challenge and question everything. When I became a teacher I taught as he had taught me, and when I became a published writer I held the same view: that the reader has to be respected and expected to 'talk themselves into being' but guided by the text, by the story, novel, poem, play, whatever.

Debby: In a real sense, then, youth literature cannot be divorced from consideration of the youth reader in the composing of youth fictions. And youth literature cannot be divorced from education.

Aidan: That's right. Youth literature, like children's literature, began as an educational tool and has developed as a distinct literature. And I've always argued that any consideration of youth literature cannot help but take into account youth readers and their responses to the fictions. It is an art that incorporates the reader in its creation and composition. And I must say I find this a fascinating aspect of the literature and of writing it. But then, I am by nature both a teacher and an author. I don't see these as different occupations but as one occupation. I'd go so far as to say I've always felt this as a singular vocation. Teaching is as much an art as authoring a novel. And I must say I've gained great satisfaction and pleasure in my sixty years of professional life from this two-in-one dedication.

A CANON AND A POETICS FOR YOUTH FICTION

Debby: We've talked a lot about youth fiction and you clearly consider it to be a distinct genre with its own poetics. If that is true, and this volume is a convincing argument that it is, what are the implications of this 'declaration' for writers, scholars and readers?

Aidan: I've argued for many years that youth fiction is a distinct literature of its own. But I'm a novelist, not an academic. I've come to this conclusion more from writing youth novels than from critical study. For many years the suggestion that it is distinct hasn't been accepted. There are signs that it is beginning to be now. There are more and more articles in specialist journals. And the book you recently mentioned to me, *Disturbing the Universe* by Roberta Seelinger Trites, is a substantial example. But by calling it 'adolescent literature' rather than young adult, which is more usual, indicates how much there is still to be done. Even the critical term for it is not yet settled. A few others have commented on the need for a canon and have suggested books that might be included. But, it seems to me, none is convincing or gives a sound basis for choice.

Debby: In the last chapter of this book, you set out what is almost a manifesto, suggesting what needs to be done.

Aidan: Yes. It seems to me a literature which is distinctly different from all others only exists if there is a canon – a list of texts which it is generally agreed anyone seriously interested should know and have read. We need this in order for there to be 'a community of similarly qualified readers,' a phrase I've adapted from Stanley Fish in his book *Is There a Text in This Class?*, where he talks about a 'community of interpretive readers'. By which I mean readers who are able to engage in intelligent, informed discussion because they share a sufficient body of references to make it possible to compare and contrast understandings of a text and construct a poetics of the genre.

Debby: I agree that a canon is essential to literary discourse, but for many years, in the study of literature as a whole, there's been considerable disagreement about what a canon is and what texts should be included. My colleague Peter Widdowson wrote well about this in his book *Literature*. He says that 'it is quite possible to accept the continued presence of the Canon – so long as it is recognised to be an artificially manufactured product within cultural history.' He acknowledges Frank Kermode's point that 'every reading list is a canon of sorts' and accepts that the 'displacement of the "great works" by hitherto disregarded ones may well substitute one canon for another.'

Aidan: I agree. But, to adapt some words of Viktor Shklovsky, where youth literature is concerned, 'There is yet no need to overthrow a canon, since there is yet no canon strong enough to be overthrown.'

Debby: There are signs a canon is emerging, though. For instance, Trites mentions texts she implies we need to know.

Aidan: She does. And she also begins a discussion of the poetics. To start with, she makes a distinction between *Bildungsroman* and *Entwicklungsroman*, suggesting that youth literature evolved from these.

Debby: *Bildungsroman* meaning stories in which the protagonist comes of age as an adult, and *Entwicklungsroman* in which the protagonist has not reached adulthood by the end of the story.

Aidan: I find that very helpful. Obviously, *The Catcher in the Rye* is an *Entwicklungsroman* whereas *Sons and Lovers* is a *Bildungsroman*. In my own fiction, I'd suggest *Dance on My Grave* is an *Entwicklungsroman* because Hal has not reached adulthood by the end, and that *This Is All* is a *Bildungsroman* because by the end both Cordelia and Will have become adults. Of course, what makes them both youth fictions rather than in the adult literary tradition is that it is the youth consciousness of the protagonists that determine the 'personality' of the narrative.

Debby: Do you have an opinion about how a canon of youth literature could be constructed?

Aidan: As I say, I'm a novelist not an academic. But for my own satisfaction I'm compiling a suggested list. It includes the following:

- **Foundation texts.** By which I mean those books from which youth literature evolved, such as Goethe's *The Sorrows of Young Werther* and Rilke's *Malte Laurids Brigg*. I doubt there'd be a lot of disagreement about these.
- **Historically important texts of youthhood.** By which I mean texts which have stood the test of time for, say, one hundred years, such as Twain's *Adventures of Huckleberry Finn* and Alcott's *Little Women*. I guess there might be some argument about this list.
- **Youthhood authors.** By which I mean texts written by authors while still in their youthhood and generally agreed to be of importance, such as Raymond Radiguet's *The Devil in the Flesh*, Anne Frank's *Diary*, and Françoise Sagan's *Bonjour Tristesse*.
- **Contemporary texts.** By which I mean those written in the previous fifty years which have not yet been sufficiently tested by the jury of time but which many agree are worthy of acceptance, such as *The Catcher in the Rye*, *The Chocolate War*, and S.E. Hinton's *The Outsiders*. This is the division about which I'd expect the most disagreement.

Debby: The examples you give are all fictions of everyday life. Do you consider that historical fiction, fantasies, science fiction, and other kinds of narrative regarded as 'young adult' belong to youth fiction as a literature of its own?

Aidan: To my mind, the types you mention are secondary. They are youth fictions provided they are narrated from a youthhood point of view and evidence the other defining features of youth fiction that I've mentioned.

Debby: Most of the contemporary texts you mention in this book are Anglo-American.

Aidan: They are. And I accept your implied criticism. They don't include texts from other English-language cultures such as Canada, Australia and New Zealand. And what we urgently need is a gathering of texts suggested by specialists from as many other languages as possible. For example, I know how strong youth literature is in Swedish, Dutch, German, and Italian. I'd very much like to know what is happening in Russia, China and Japan and elsewhere. Are there Arabic youth fictions, for example?

Debby: How could this be done?

Aidan: Perhaps IBBY or the IRSCL or an interested university or some other suitable institution could organise a conference that brings together specialists from many languages precisely for the purpose of formulating a tentative international canon of youth literature.

Debby: That would be good. But I can see a problem. In order for a canon to exist the texts included in it must be available for everyone who is interested. And the fact is that British and American publishing does not include many translations; often no more than one or two per cent of the youth books published are translations, whereas it is thirty or forty per cent in some European countries.

Aidan: You're right. As you know, I've been banging on for years about the need in Britain and the US for more translations of children's and youth fiction. So the conference would have to include discussion of how key texts from these many languages can be translated into other languages that have so far ignored them. There could be a solution to this in Europe, where I believe there is unused money available for translations, at least for languages within the EU.

Debby: And once a canon has been established?

Aidan: A distinct literature has its own poetics. Again, we need scholarly academics to produce a study of its poetics.

Debby: How do you think this would help or influence authors, publishers and readers of youth literature?

Aidan: It's noticeable historically how artistic innovation and development go hand in hand with a lot of vibrant criticism. The one stimulates the other. And this influences authors. It encourages them – gives them permission, if you like – to do more, take risks, experiment, and develop their work. This in turn encourages publishers to take risks. And this provides readers with a wider, richer choice, which in turn expands the readership.

References

Roland Barthes, *The Preparation of the Novel*, trans. Kate Briggs, Columbia University Press, 2011. Pages 146, 132, 137.

Aidan Chambers, *Tell Me: Children, Reading & Talk with The Reading Environment*, Thimble Press, 2011. Page 132.

Aidan Chambers, *The Toll Bridge*, Bodley Head, 1992. Page 192.

George Eliot, 'The Natural History of German Life' (1856), quoted in James Wood, *How Fiction Works*, Jonathan Cape, 2008. Page 129-30.

Johann Wolfgang von Goethe, *The Sufferings of Young Werther* (1774), trans. Stanley Corngold, W.W. Norton, 2012

Wolfgang Iser, *The Implied Reader: A Theory of Aesthetic Response*, Routledge & Kegan Paul, 1978

Frank Kermode, quoted in Peter Widdowson, *Literature*, Routledge, 1999. Page 23.

Milan Kundera, *Writers at Work: The Paris Review Interviews*, Seventh Series, ed. George Plimpton, Secker & Warburg, 1987. Page 219.

Philip Roth, *Writers at Work: The Paris Review Interviews*, Seventh Series, ed. George Plimpton, Secker & Warburg, 1987

Jean-Paul Sartre, *What Is Literature?*, trans. Bernard Frechtman (1948), Routledge, 2001. Pages 33-4, 41, 32-3.

Viktor Shklovsky, *The Theory of Prose*, trans. Benjamin Sher, Dalkey Archive Press (1990), 1991. Pages 6, 203.

Peter Widdowson, *Literature*, Routledge, 1999. Page 23.

Ludwig Wittgenstein, *Culture and Value*, trans. Peter Winch, ed. G.H. von Wright with Heikki Nyman, Basil Blackwell, 1980. Page 74e.

Ludwig Wittgenstein, *Philosophical Investigations*, trans. G.E.M. Anscombe, Basil Blackwell, 1958. Page viii.

WS - #0177 - 301120 - C0 - 216/138/11 - PB - 9781916121409

31. Father, deliver me from any ignorance of y workings in my life. In the name of Jesus.

32. Father, help me that I may not take your mercy in life for granted. In the name of Jesus.

33. Father, by your favour, deliver me from affliction the name of Jesus.

34. Father, by your favour, prevent me from failure. In name of Jesus.

35. Father, by your favour, reverse every downward tre in my life. In the name of Jesus.

36. Father, by your favour, take me beyond my drea In the name of Jesus.

37. Father, by your favour, turn my dream into reality the name of Jesus.

38. Father, by your favour, end stagnation in my life the name of Jesus.

Time of Favour

Father, as Lot found favour with you and was delivered:
from imminent danger, deliver me from every danger. In the name of Jesus.

Father, as Abraham found favour with you and hosted heavenly visitors, make my home a place of visitation for heavenly hosts. In the name of Jesus.

Father, as Sarah found favour with you and her doubt could not hinder her miracle, remove every personal barrier between me and my miracle. In the name of Jesus.

Father, let my path shine forever with your favour. In the name of Jesus.

Father, grant me unforgettable divine encounters with your favour. In the name of Jesus.

Father, by your favour grant me to inherit the labour of the gentiles. In the name of Jesus.

Father, by your favour take me beyond the limit set by my enemies. In the name of Jesus.

Time of Favour

46. Father, in your favour open my eyes to behold your glory as you did for Moses. In the name of Jesus.

47. Father, by your favour, give me the miracle that eluded me for years. In the name of Jesus.

48. Father, by your favour, let there be restoration in life. In the name of Jesus.

49. Father, in your favour, stop the mouth of my enemy against me. In the name of Jesus.

50. Father, in your favour, let goodness and mercy follow my life forever. In the name of Jesus.

otes